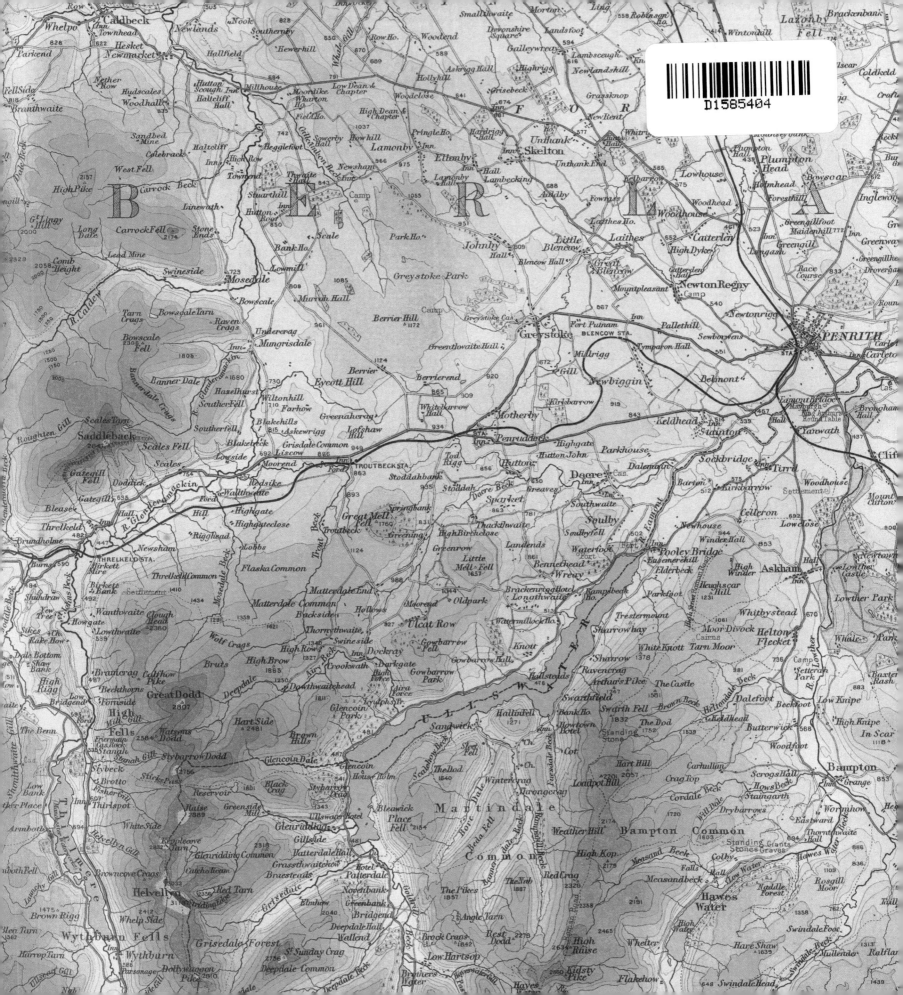

THE
ENGLISH LAKES

· MEMORIES OF TIMES PAST ·

· 75 PAINTINGS BY ALFRED HEATON COOPER ·

INTRODUCTION BY BILL BIRKETT AND JANE RENOUF
TEXT BY COLIN INMAN AND ROSEMARY ANDERSON

A NOTE TO THE READER

In order to keep the pages of the book as uncluttered as possible, all sources, notes and captions relating to illustrations other than the main paintings have been grouped at the end of the book, and will be found on pages 169–71.

The endpapers are taken from *The Survey Atlas of England and Wales,* drawn, engraved, printed and published at The Edinburgh Geographical Institute in 1903.

First published in the UK in 2006 by Worth Press Ltd, Cambridge, United Kingdom.
Reprinted 2008

Project manager   John Button
Design managers   Lucy Guenot and Catherine Smith

Set in Centaur and Gill Sans by Bookcraft Ltd, Stroud, Gloucestershire
Printed in China by Imago

A Memories of Times Past title
www.memoriesoftimespast.com

ISBN   978 1 903025 44 4

CONTENTS

THE ENGLISH LAKES 1905

BILL BIRKETT AND JANE RENOUF

Alfred Heaton Cooper's sparkling qualities as a painter of mountain landscape a century ago might have remained in relative obscurity – had it not been for Edwardian England's growing hunger for leisure and holidaymaking.

This was a period of considerable social change in Britain, as the nation, built on strict social order, ingenuity, hard work, industrial and military might, began to let its hair down. Daringly this little island country, whose Empire and influence stretched around the globe, began to tolerate the working classes taking an annual, though as yet unpaid, holiday. It was the birth of mass tourism and the opportunity for Alfred, the gifted son of working-class parents to realise his

talent and dreams, uproot from the industrial grime of Bolton, and literally set up shop in beautiful Lakeland.

To see bustling little Lakeland towns and villages thronged with visitors nowadays, people might mistakenly think tourism arrived with cars and motorways – but the story started much earlier than that. Lakeland tourism dates back to the mid 1700s when those wealthy enough to own a carriage, and brave enough to risk perilous passes and rutted tracks, came in fashionable pursuit of nature and the 'picturesque', based largely on European Romanticism. As visiting numbers increased, roads were improved and new roadside inns built – but it was the presence of Wordsworth and other famous romantics which steered tourism into the 19th century, and brought ever more followers, seeking rustic simplicity amidst scenic magnificence. Those who had once embarked on the Grand European tour now found their travels curtailed by war and revolution – but the Lake District provided a far safer alternative and the outpourings of its poets sold by the thousand. Artists, too, had turned to nature, and landscape painting became increasingly popular throughout the century.

Travel, once the preserve of a wealthy elite, suddenly lay within reach of millions. Turnpike roads and faster, safer and more frequent stagecoach services speeded up journey times. By the 1840s and 50s, hotels and boarding

houses were springing up in all the major Lakeland towns to accommodate not only the wealthy but also the new and prosperous middle classes. However it was the arrival of the railway, planned primarily for industry, which opened the door to mass tourism and helped the Lakes to become somewhere that everyone could enjoy, rich or poor. Thanks to passenger trains, its clean fresh air and sparkling waters lay within a couple of hours of most northern industrial towns — the perfect place to find relief from the smoke, squalor and disease in which mill and factory workers lived and worked. Their wealthy bosses went one step further and bought their own little corners of Lakeland, building ornate villas and extravagant country houses as second homes.

A number of independent railway companies built lines and stations which were to nurture and harvest the blossoming tourist industry. Suddenly the region was not only open to day visitors from the nearby northern industrial towns but to travellers from London, the latter reaching the Lakes within some 8 hours of boarding the train at Euston. Leading the march came the Kendal and Windermere Railway Company with the construction of Windermere Station in 1847.

A photochrome showing Bowness boat landing in the early 1900s

An advertisement for paddle steamer and rail trips taken from an *Album of Views* photographed and published by G.P. Abraham of Keswick in 1911 (left). Enjoying refreshment outside Kentmere Church in 1906 (above).

The very name of this new station was, in point of fact, one of the first marketing ploys of the railways to sell tourism. "Windermere Station" was actually situated in the small hamlet of Birthwaite, some two miles away from the shores of England's largest and most famous lake, Windermere. Of course the newly found "Windermere" did provide relatively easy access to the lake and its steamers. In consequence "Windermere" became synonymous with the lake and was rapidly to burgeon in size, importance and public recognition whilst the name Birthwaite quietly slipped out of use.

Similarly the West Coast line of "Whitehaven and Furness," also completed in 1847 and later to become part of the London and North Western Railway (LNWR), provided access to the remote dales, deep lakes, and high mountains of Wasdale and Ennerdale.

Penrith, situated on the Lancaster and Carlisle line, served the eastern lakes and Ullswater Lake in particular. With the completion of stations at Coniston in 1859 and Keswick in 1865, rail access opened all doors to the magic of the Lakes. The railway companies were quick to promote their wares and the London main line stations, particularly those of the LNER and LMS, sported attractive and alluring posters advertising the virtues of England's beautiful Lake District.

By Edwardian times, many workers were taking an unpaid annual holiday. People would put money into friendly societies and savings clubs all year to pay for a week's jollity and, in many mill towns, businesses closed down in unison, releasing a great flood of weary workers in search of recreation. Whilst many pleasure seekers headed for Blackpool, the more serious minded, energetic and adventurous found the Lakes more attractive, and it was also favourite for Sunday School and Church outings. The popularity of bicycling provided thrills and spills galore, and jolly parties of young men and women wobbled along the lanes and

passengers climbed up a little ladder and sat on top, which could be a very damp experience indeed in bad weather. Fully-laden coaches couldn't get up the steeper hills, so people were expected to get off and walk from time to time. Local children delighted in opening farm gates or chasing coaches downhill, in the hope visitors would throw them tuppence to buy a bar of Fry's chocolate cream or five Woodbines. Coaches went all over the Lakes as well as out to the west coast, visiting Morecambe Bay, Broughton and the Furness Peninsula. Edwardians loved fanciful tales of sprites and fairies, and visitors flocked to romantic landmarks steeped in legend such as ancient ivy-clad ruins and fairy grottoes. One of the Low Wood Hotel's most popular coach trips crossed on board the Windermere ferry heading for the wishing well at Humphrey Head, the tallest limestone cliff in Cumbria with panoramic views of Morecambe Bay sands. The legend that the last wolf in England was reputedly killed there in the 15th century just added to the day's excitement.

Although coaches served all the main routes, visitors in remoter hamlets depended on whatever means of transport they could find to get to the station or catch a boat. Even the most badly repaired farm carts were brought into service to carry trippers, and though mishaps occurred, most were not too serious. One Langdale farmer was even reputed to be the only man in England to unseat three Members of Parliament

A photochrome of the Windermere steam ferry (above). Kendal Zion chapel choir outing in 1907 (right). The coaches and drivers were hired from Rigg's of Windermere.

brought welcome custom to country inns and tearooms. Even the lowliest paid could afford a ride on a steamer, or to hire a rowing boat and take the family fishing for the day.

Once people arrived, touring the Lakes was popularly done by horse-drawn coach, and many hotels ran stagecoach services to take the visitors on to see the sights and visit the famous lakes, dales and fells. Richard Rigg was based at the Windermere Hotel and operated black and yellow horse-drawn coaches with the drivers, wearing top hats and red coats, becoming known as the Robin Red Breasts. Before the advent of the motor car, Rigg's maintained 200 horses each tourist season and many other hotels stabled upwards of 60 horses to run their own "four in hand" coaches. Some of the drivers were notorious local characters, whose driving exploits were as notable as their early-morning drinking sessions, standing outside the big hotels as they touted for business. To board a "four in hand",

in one day! The unfortunate trio were returning to Windermere Station after a rock climbing holiday when the string securing the rickety old cart broke, tipping them all into the road with their luggage.

In the earliest years of the century, the sight or sound of a car on a Lakeland street was an occasion of such rarity that people would rush out to take a look. Only the very rich could afford cars and motoring conditions were far from ideal. In pre-tarmacadam days, many Lakeland roads were surfaced with sammell, which was dug out from roadside pits. This orange-coloured subsoil mixed with small stones provided quite a firm surface, but often needed to be watered in summer to keep the dust down and soon filled with puddles in winter. Some locals found it hard to imagine motors would ever replace horses and even questioned the usefulness of anything that went as slowly as a car, broke down as frequently, or left ladies' costumes quite so dusty or muddy. Without doubt it was the "Thousand Miles Trial" held in 1900 and organised by the Automobile Club (later to become the RAC) that most notably brought the motor car to the attention of the wider British public. On passing through the Lake District it was reported in the local *Westmorland Gazette* newspaper that: "The passage through Ambleside created an unusual amount of interest, and the streets along the line of route were thronged with people who had left their occupations to witness the novelty. The children at both the boys' and girls' schools had holiday."

It was little wonder that the 1900 Trial attracted so much excitement, considering there were only an estimated 800 cars in use in the whole of Britain. Three years later, Henry Ford sold his first motorcar in America, and the idea of motorised transport for the masses captured the popular imagination on both sides of the Atlantic. There is little doubt that by 1905, the year the AA was founded, the motor car was beginning to cause a noticeable increase in tourism throughout the Lakes. The Edwardian era was a period of phenomenal growth in road traffic, and by 1914 there were some 132,000 cars on Britain's roads.

The combustion engine soon made its impact on public transport, though the first regular bus service running in 1904 between Windermere and Grasmere via Ambleside bus depot used steam buses fired up by paraffin. The journey took forty minutes when everything ran to plan, though admittedly on occasions, with much cheering and jeering, these buses were passed

23 April 1900: a motor car on the "Thousand Miles Trial" – a car run from Hyde Park to Kendal – arrives in Kendal. The man standing and saluting in the car is the Hon. C.S. Rolls, who founded the Rolls-Royce company in 1906.

Low Wood Hotel, Windermere

PRINCE of WALES
LAKE HOTEL,
GRASMERE.

Delightfully situated on the shore of the Lake, near Dove
Cottage, the early home of Wordsworth, and Grasmere Church.
R.A.C., A.A., and M.U.

"The loveliest spot that man hath ever found."—WORDSWORTH.

THE ONLY HOTEL ON THE LAKE.

FISHING AND BOATING.

Garage.] VIEW OF HOTEL FROM THE LAKE. **[Petrol.**

Coaches Daily to Keswick, Ullswater, Langdales, Coniston, Winder-
mere, and round Thirlmere. *Direct pony-tracks* to Easedale Tarn,
Borrowdale, Derwentwater, Ullswater, and the tops of Helvellyn and
Fairfield.
Communication by Through Trains:—
From **London** (by L. & N.W.R. to Windermere, and thence by motor or coach)
in 7½ hrs.
"   "   (by Midland and Furness Railways, and up Lake Windermere), in 8 hrs.

Telegrams—"Prince Hotel, Grasmere."   **J. COWPERTHWAITE,**
Telephone No. 4, Grasmere.   PROPRIETOR.

be glad to take in one or two visitors, however cramped. Few houses had running water, let alone flush toilets or baths, and visitors shared the outdoor earth closet with the family — and maybe a neighbouring one too. Food was generous, with four good meals a day: porridge and cream, home-cured ham and eggs, roasts, steamed puddings and pies, apple and currant pasties and turnovers, slabs of gingerbread, farmhouse cheeses with freshly baked bread and farm butter, pickles and chutney. Alternatively, many visitors who took rooms would bring in or buy their own food, which they gave to the landlady to cook and serve. Many visitors were loyal customers and would return to the same "digs", year after year.

There were no visitor or tourist information centres a century ago, so people had to rely on books to discover the attractions of the area, as had been the way for over 100 years, since the first popular *Guide to the Lakes* was published in 1778 by the Jesuit priest, Father Thomas West. Others followed, notably William Wordsworth's *Guide to the Lakes* in 1810, and *The Tourist's New Guide* by the Ambleside artist, William Green in 1819. Their rich prose whetted the public's imagination, but the words had to be particularly colourful and descriptive to make up for the monochrome illustrations which left much to the imagination. All this was to change with the introduction of colour illustrations in the early 1900s. These not only served as guides to where people might visit, but also made the perfect little gift or souvenir. Few visitors could afford to buy an original painting as a souvenir, as poor Alfred Heaton Cooper had found to his cost, but buying a guidebook packed with richly printed colour illustrations of favourite Lakeland haunts was quite a different matter. Lavish colour pictures lent new romance to lakes and crags and as opportunities increased to enjoy exciting new pursuits such as fell walking, rock climbing and bicycle touring, the market for guidebooks grew apace.

Blackie & Son Limited published their *Cumberland,*

by horse-drawn coaches! By 1910 one or two astute locals set up taxi services using Model-T Fords. They travelled at such a leisurely pace that Grasmere's taxi driver was reputed to keep a shotgun handy under his seat, so he could pot the occasional pheasant whenever the opportunity arose.

Finding somewhere suitable to stay was never too difficult, despite the absence of "bed and breakfast" signs so familiar today. There were hotels for the better off, and no shortage of lodging houses for "paying guests" or "holiday visitors" who wanted to stay a few weeks. Finding short-stay accommodation was rather more of a gamble and might involve taking pot luck on a pier or station platform. Mothers would send their children down to meet boats and trains, brandishing boards marked up with their rates, but cheaper accommodation could usually be found in smaller villages by simply knocking on cottage doors. Families who found it hard to make ends meet would

Westmorland and Furness in 1905 at the princely price of "Eight Pence" and it proved to be very popular. Easy to slip into the pocket, it described the principal attractions of the area typically: "Windermere is 10½ miles long and varies from ¼ of a mile to 1¼ miles in breadth. The upper or northern half is more picturesque."

Another pocket sized guide, *The English Lake District* compiled by J B Baddeley was published by Ward Lock & Co Ltd and contained "19 coloured contour maps by J. Bartholomew". This was a real tour de force and a must-have publication for any visitor to the region. It contained general information as diverse as "Geology" and "Ice and Snow Sports", and included in-depth analysis of town and village with wonderfully detailed descriptions of walks and events to be found at each locality.

Baddeley noted that: "The winters in the Lake District are often extremely severe and splendid skating is to be had on many of the lakes". For the "Orrest Head" walk above Windermere he boldly states it is: "The finest extensive viewpoint in the Lake District, and, perhaps, the finest in Great Britain." He illustrates the point further by having a fold out panorama map identifying the heights all around.

These guidebooks were carried in the pocket and used in conjunction with the excellent foldaway sheet maps printed on cloth. The latter included the 1 inch to the mile Ordnance Survey Map and the beautifully coloured John Bartholomew & Son Ltd maps in two scales – one inch and half inch to the mile.

With visitor numbers ever increasing, services were constantly adapting to accommodate the fleeting summer influx and in 1905, Coniston Station extended the length of the platform to take longer excursion trains, and added a new refreshment room. For a village formerly known for its mining and quarrying rather than as a holiday resort, tourism was changing the landscape. Even though Coniston still only had two residential hotels, there were no fewer than five refreshment rooms and 14 lodging houses at that time, supported by a network of private houses and farms

Cover and interior spread from *The English Lakes*, 12 chromo views and a guide book, published by T. Nelson and Sons in about 1902.

also catering for tourists. Although the season only lasted from Whitsun to the beginning of September, over 20,000 people cruised on Coniston's steam yacht Gondola that summer.

With just a few brief weeks to benefit from summer visitors, local entrepreneurs had never been short of novel money-making ideas. Visitors could hire a guide and ascend Helvellyn by pony from Grasmere, or be taken to see a mountain sunrise. Private landowners often charged the public to see sights of natural wonder such as waterfalls, and at Ambleside's Stock Ghyll Falls visitors entered by putting a penny in the turnstile. There were teas in the refreshment shelter and gentleman were permitted to bathe under the falls early in the morning or late evening – towels provided.

Photographic prints and postcards of local scenes and beauty spots were incredibly popular and each tourist centre had a number of flourishing photographic businesses ready to capture the spirit of the age. In Keswick the Abraham Brothers, using great cameras

10016. - BORROWDALE VALLEY.

Photochrome of the Borrowdale valley.

the photographs of this lethal looking biplane which are the most memorable. Ambleside photographers included the Mayson Brothers and Bells, all recording this vibrant period of Lakeland history.

By Edwardian times fell walking was long established and routes to the highest mountains, Helvellyn, Skiddaw, The Langdale Pikes and Scafell Pike, highest point in England, were thronged with people. Tea houses, now long gone or ruinous, were a common feature beside the most popular paths notably at beauty spots such as Easedale Tarn above Grasmere or even on the very summit of Scafell Pike. Impressive waterfalls which are now mainly forgotten, typically the dramatic drops of Scale Force behind Crummock Water, Great Langdale's Dungeon Ghyll and Ambleside's Stock Ghyll Force, were all made accessible by ladder and walkway in this exciting age of discovery and adventure.

It was, too, the golden age of rock climbing and mountaineering. Reflecting the growth and popularity of the sport one of Britain's most prestigious climbing clubs, The Fell and Rock Climbing Club of the English Lake District, was formed in Keswick in 1906. Although O G Jones, whose book *Rock Climbing In The English Lake District*, was first published in 1897, had already departed (pulled to his death by a falling guide in the Swiss Alps in 1899), his influence lingered on and it was his great friends, George

of brass and mahogany and recording onto glass plates, produced wonderful images of the high fells and climbing in both summer and winter. Particularly striking were those of the Napes Needle and Sphinx Rock with Edwardian climbers sporting nailed boots and the ladies still wearing full length skirts. Early motor cars making precipitous ascent and descent of the mountain passes, Dunmail, Kirkstone, Honister, Newlands, Whinlatter, Wrynose and Hardnott were also favourite subjects. A few doors away from the great Abraham emporium the Maysons specialised in photographing sylvan Borrowdale and the Derwent Water regattas.

Similarly in Bowness, Brunskill's of Lake Road went out onto the ice of frozen Lake Windermere to record the hundreds of skaters in action. In 1912 twenty-two-year-old Frank Herbert, possibly the most daring of them all, took aerial photographs from a bamboo framed "waterplane" named Water Hen. Actually it is

and Ashley Abraham, who founded the FRCC. Their photographs and books are still regarded as amongst the most influential ever to be produced on the subject.

Of course, not everyone came in search of energetic adventure. For those preferring parks and gentle promenades, indoor entertainment was in short supply on rainy days, which must have made the 1906 opening of Keswick's Museum and Art Gallery in Fitz Park a red-letter day. Yet the busy streets themselves provided plenty of spectacle, with everything from itinerant performers to temperance bands. Small visiting circuses or menageries occasionally came in summer and drew the crowds with dancing bears, performing dogs, and monkeys on sticks. Open carts hung with their wares trundled the lanes, and even the scissor grinder was a sight to see, kitted out in a smart top hat as he reddled away sharpening knives at his flower-painted workbench. In common with villages the length and breadth of the land, most little Lakeland communities had flourishing church choirs and brass or silver bands, and enjoyed flower festivals and tableaux and numerous celebrations of empire. Added to this, popular local sports including wrestling, guides races up the fells and hound trailing delighted visitors who had saved so hard all year and were anxious not to miss a single attraction.

For the more highbrow, there were concerts, music festivals, light operetta, country dancing and amateur theatricals in even the smallest places. However few entertainments in Edwardian times surpassed the excitement of the visiting cinematograph, which replaced the popular magic lantern shows of Victorian times. From the early 1900s, thousands in Britain flocked to see short films of quite ordinary, everyday events, such was their novelty. Films were accompanied by a pianist – and in Ambleside, the accompanist drew full houses with his version of a ragtime cowboy show. Coniston showed short films in its Institute, projected on to a sheet. The cinema visited twice a week from Barrow and broke down frequently, much to the

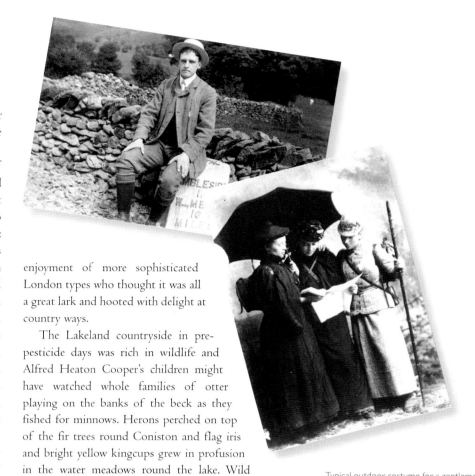

enjoyment of more sophisticated London types who thought it was all a great lark and hooted with delight at country ways.

The Lakeland countryside in pre-pesticide days was rich in wildlife and Alfred Heaton Cooper's children might have watched whole families of otter playing on the banks of the beck as they fished for minnows. Herons perched on top of the fir trees round Coniston and flag iris and bright yellow kingcups grew in profusion in the water meadows round the lake. Wild flowers were so plentiful, people thought nothing of picking them by the armful.

Alfred's few diaries indicate that he was always impressed by wealthy patronage, and hoped to make good sales – and the Lake District's popularity with aristocracy and the intelligentsia would have given him high hopes. The country house weekend was an extravagant feature of Edwardian society generally, but many of the larger Lakeland houses where such parties were hosted were only used for about two months in summer, though they maintained a retinue of staff throughout the year. One wealthy manufacturing family visiting their large Hawkshead mansion from Newcastle regularly hired a carriage on the train to bring the servants, their coach and horses and trunks packed with the second-best silver and linen, just for a few brief weeks. Country houses held garden parties and dinners on an elaborate scale, with crates of lobster

Typical outdoor costume for a gentleman in the Lakes in 1905 (left). Three ladies set out on a walk c.1900 (above).

Camping at Windermere (top) – note the cups and saucers! Children working at Phillipson's of Spark Bridge in 1899 (above). They are sitting at bobbin-roughing machines.

and strawberries arriving fresh by train that day from London markets. Shooting parties were rarer, but hospitality was just as lavish, with lunch laid out high up in the hills in the shooting box. A farmer's daughter from Rydal recalled that, around 1906, the big Hall employed 32 staff when the Squire was at home. This included the ordinary governess and the French governess, a nanny and an under nurse, several butlers and footmen, three house maids, the housekeeper, the kitchen and scullery maids, three woodmen, three gamekeepers, and a liveried coachman and groom. As cars become more commonly used, grooms and coachmen became chauffeurs and the stables were converted into garages. Fashionable winter resorts in Edwardian days included Monte Carlo and the Riviera, and one Grasmere chauffeur in 1912 sailed from Tilbury to Marseilles with the car, to get it to the south of France as quickly as possible.

The gulf between rich and poor was wide, and Edwardian politics and world events had little impact on ordinary lives in the Lake District. Although there were two postal deliveries a day, world news was slow to travel up isolated valleys and communications were scanty. In 1901, as Marconi made the first transatlantic radio communication, Lakeland news travelled rather slower via gossip at the weekly market or the hiring fair. Few people took a daily paper until World War 1 and anyone wanting to know what was going on in the world would visit the penny reading room, where there might be a single, dog-eared newspaper provided.

Even the growing boldness of suffragettes in towns and cities attracted little local interest. In 1903, the year when Emmeline Pankhurst founded her Women's Social and Political Union, Lakeland women had little time or energy to fight for the vote. There would have been few farmers' wives or landladies among the onlookers as the daughters of an educated and wealthy elite campaigned at various public meetings in the area. However, although women would have to wait many more years before they could vote, emancipation advanced slowly but relentlessly. These were the early days of women's mountaineering, tennis and cycling ... despite large hats with plumes and feathers. A suffragette was even arrested in Bowness. Not much, but from small acorns large oaks do grow. Beatrix Potter, whose considerable contribution to natural history was ignored by the all-male elite, soon found fame and fortune instead as author in 1902 of *The Tale of Peter Rabbit*, which remains a world best-seller.

Lakeland families were large, often with as many as ten children. With many mouths to feed, working twelve hour days, six days a week, was commonplace. With a plentiful labour force to supply the many industries of slate quarrying, mineral mining, bobbin mills, gunpowder mills, pencil factories, wood yards, charcoal burning and iron manufacture, the production of agricultural machinery and agriculture itself, the largest employer of them all, wages were kept low. A skilled worker in industry could expect around £1 per week whilst a girl on a farm as little as £5 for a half year.

Nobody could possibly have predicted how the innovators, designers and great thinkers at work in the first few years of the 20th century would re-shape their world, and lay down the blueprint for ours. It was a golden moment in time, when Britain still ruled the waves in military might, trade and industry. However, the glory of Edwardian England was all too short-lived – the most horrific war in history would soon fragment society and erode traditional values.

Amidst such change, one aspect of Lakeland remains unaltered from that time to this. The landscape is as glorious and beautiful as ever it was in Alfred Heaton Cooper's day, and his illustrations are just as true and faithful a representation of the splendours of the Lake District as the day they were painted.

ALFRED HEATON COOPER
1863–1929

COLIN INMAN

Alfred Heaton Cooper was born on 14 June 1863 in Swinton, Manchester, although his later passports opt for a date a year later. His parents both worked in the cotton industry: his father William Cooper was a cashier and his wife Alice a weaver.

Alfred was the second of six children born over a period of 16 years but the oldest to survive infancy: an elder sister had died when three months old.

His parents made great efforts to educate their children well – three of them went on to make successful careers in the worlds of painting and photography.

Alfred left school at 14 to work as a clerk at Bolton Town Hall. But his artistic ability was already apparent in his sketches and paintings of the countryside around his home, and in the early 1880s his mother encouraged him to send work to London and try to win a place at art college. In this he was successful, moving to London in 1884 to study under George Clausen at a time of challenge and change in Western European art. He was heavily influenced by Turner and Constable at this time.

His first picture for exhibition at the Royal Academy summer exhibition was accepted in 1887 and he continued to send pictures there from time to time until 1925.

He lived at first in Chelsea and later at Windsor, sketching and painting scenes in London and along the Thames. However, in 1889, after a long holiday in Morocco and Gibraltar, he returned north again, living near Grassington and spending time retracing Turner's journey through the beauty spots of Yorkshire.

In 1891 Alfred Heaton Cooper moved for a time to Norway, a country that fascinated him for the rest of his life. His aim was to sell paintings to the tourists who were increasingly visiting the area. For some time he lodged at the home of Rasmus Valentinsen, a wool dyer, where he fell in love with one of the daughters, Mathilde Marie. But by 1892 Alfred was forced for financial reasons to leave Norway and return home. On his return he wrote proposing to Mathilde and explaining that it would take him at least a year to save enough money to be able to marry her. She accepted his offer and said she was willing to wait. Eventually he had saved enough and set off for Norway again, where the wedding took place in Tjugum Church in the autumn of 1894.

By November the couple were back in England, living near Bolton. Following the death of their first child, Sverre, at only six months, they moved again, to Southport. A daughter, Ellide, was born there in 1897.

Eventually money problems and the need to live somewhere with cleaner air for the sake of his wife's

While baby is asleep – Mathilde with Ellide drawn in 1897 (top). Alfred and Mathilde in front of The Log House, also known as The Norwegian Studio, in Coniston in 1913 (right). The Log House (above).

health forced another move, this time to the Lake District, where the climate was nearer to that of Mathilde's native Norway, and it was here that Heaton Cooper found the ideal subject for his art as well as a regular procession of tourists whom he hoped would buy his work. The family lived first at Hawkshead and later at The Gate House, Coniston, on the bank of Mines Beck. The house was soon renamed Solheim, but is now called The Gate House again. Here two boys were born, Frithjof in 1900 and in 1903 William, who himself became well known as a Lake District painter.

The commission from publisher A&C Black in 1904 to produce 75 illustrations for *The English Lakes* transformed the family's fortunes, and Alfred continued to provide illustrations for their books for the rest of his life, some 400 in total.

Lacking a suitable studio, Alfred decided to have one built in Norway and import it to Coniston: there were few planning regulations at the time to prevent him from doing this; today there would be no chance! In the event the cost of transport was greater than that of the building itself. It was erected behind the Crown Hotel and used as a gallery to exhibit and sell his pictures, an arrangement that drew some criticism from established artists in the area. Alfred stood at a distance from the Lake Artists Society and its members for most of his life.

Following the completion of the A&C Black commission, the family moved back to Balholm in Norway for a time and on the shore of Sognefjord erected a similar log cabin structure to the Coniston one but bigger. This was used as both home and studio and was known as the Cooperhus. It still exists today. But once again the failure to sell enough pictures forced a move back to England in 1908, where they lived for a time at Ulverston, where a daughter Una was born, before a final move was made to Ambleside in 1912. There were more tourists visiting Ambleside and therefore more potential buyers. The Norwegian studio was re-erected at Ambleside, plank by numbered plank, and moved a final time in 1928 to the south end of the village, where it still stands today.

Alfred continued to illustrate books, among them *The Isle of Wight* (1908), *The Isle of Man* (1909), *Norfolk and Suffolk* (1921), *Dorset* (1925), *Somerset* (1927). In 1907 he made his only foray into authorship with *The Norwegian Fjords*, published in A&C Black's Six Shilling Series and later reissued with abridged text in the Beautiful Britain series. He seems not to have enjoyed doing so: his son William reported that he said he would never write another book, and he didn't. In 1919 he provided illustrations for a *20 Shilling Series* book on Ireland, a curious commission since the book had been previously been issued with what seemed to be adequate illustrations by Francis Walker. It is possible to speculate that the publisher helped him out at a time of financial stringency.

As William has pointed out, Alfred's best work is not necessarily to be found in the books: they placed restrictions on him by requiring that he tailor his art to the text of various authors and to the needs of the colour plate process used to reproduce them: A&C Black found it easiest to deal with originals of about 8 by 12 inches. That Alfred's range was wider than depicted in the books can be seen from the illustrations in Jane Renouf's biography.

The family's final home at Ambleside was Cross Brow, a 17th century cottage. Alfred continued to walk and paint while Mathilde ran the studio. He was particularly fond of painting while his friend A. Holden Illingworth fished for trout or salmon, and his paintings appear in two books of Illingworth's reminiscences. In the 1920s he also visited Denmark, Sweden, Derbyshire, Durham and Northumberland for book illustrations. He paid his last visit to Norway in 1927, where he painted at Bergen, Tromsø and the Lofoten Islands.

Sometime during 1928 Alfred became ill with stomach cancer. He was operated on in June 1929 but died at his home on 21 July at the age of 66. He was

buried at St Mary's Parish Church, Ambleside. Mathilde survived him by 24 years, dying at the age of 90 in 1953; she was buried beside him.

Anyone interested in finding out more can be directed to *Alfred Heaton Cooper: Painter of Landscape* by Jane Renouf, published by Red Bank Press in 1997 and available from the Heaton Cooper Studio. This is a lavishly illustrated and well written biography, to which I am indebted for much of the information outlined above.

Alfred's family continue to paint in the Lake District today and they also run the Heaton Cooper gallery and shop, in Grasmere, which was built by Alfred's son William in 1938. Here original paintings and prints by Alfred, William and Alfred's grandchildren can be viewed and purchased. Alfred would doubtless be surprised to find that his paintings today sell for thousands of pounds.

Many of Alfred's paintings can be found at the Bolton Art Gallery, and there is a changing exhibition of his works at Grasmere.

Hay cutting, Grasmere (above). Pencil sketch (below) of an old field gate near Esthwaite.

PLATE 1

A MISTY MORNING, NEWBY BRIDGE, WINDERMERE

Newby Bridge crosses the River Leven near the south end
of Windermere; it also lends its name to the adjacent hamlet.

The first wooden bridge to be built over the river here was called New Bridge. Then, in the 1630s, a more substantial wooden bridge was built, but the constant use of these bridges for transporting timber meant that they soon wore out. The present one, a packhorse-style stone bridge of five arches, was built between 1651 and 1652. A letter from the builders quotes a price of £90 for a stone and £60 for a wooden bridge; it goes on to point out that a wooden bridge would wear quicker and would soon be destroyed by the transporting of timber across it. Since a stone bridge would obviously benefit the local merchant families who sponsored it, that is what was built. The sponsors' names are inscribed underneath one of the arches.

The prosperity of the area was ensured at the turn of the 19th century by several industries, including the production of charcoal – the region being ideal for this, having a scant population and many trees – and the manufacture of gunpowder, which lasted until the end of World War I. Among other industries were the bobbin mills, and the railway which brought tourism to the Lakes.

PLATE 2

FURNESS ABBEY IN THE VALE OF NIGHTSHADE

The name, Vale of Nightshade, derives from a nearby valley that was overgrown with deadly nightshade, also known as belladonna, a plant with very poisonous berries.

The Abbey is of red sandstone and the ruins bear witness to its importance as one of England's most powerful monastic settlements from Norman times until its dissolution in 1537. The Abbey's Cistercian monks owned vast tracts of land in Furness and the Lake District, transforming rough pastures to productive sheep grazing, and harvesting timber to produce charcoal for the smelting of iron. It was Victorian entrepreneurs, or "profane despoilers" as Wordsworth would have it, who, perhaps not surprisingly, routed the Furness Railway close to the Abbey

Ruins – though even Wordsworth had to acknowledge that the Abbey's spiritual aura remained intact:

Railway Labourers …
They sit, they walk
Among the ruins but no idle talk is heard …
All seem to feel the spirit of the place,
And by the general reverence God is praised;
Profane Despoilers, stand ye not reproved,
While thus these simple hearted men are moved?

PLATE 3

WINDERMERE FROM WANSFELL (SUNSET)

Wansfell, rising to nearly 500 metres above Ambleside, has always been the perfect vantage point
from which to view the expanse of Windermere, the longest of the National Park's lakes.

John Dalton.

Eaglesfield near Workington;
many of his ideas were developed
during summer holidays in the
Lakes. In August 1831 he and his
companion Jonathan Otley, author of
the much-reprinted *Otley's Lakeland Guide*,
ascended Wansfell from Low Wood Inn. From the summit they
had "charming views of Windermere, with its many wood-clad
islets". The same view led Wordsworth to write, in *The Prelude*,
Book 4:

Like most placenames in the Lake District, both Wansfell and
Windermere have their origins in Old Norse – possibly Woden's
Fell after the Norse god of death, wisdom and magic, and
Vinandr's Lake, Vinandr being a fairly common Old Swedish
personal name.

William Wordsworth always referred to the lake as
Winandermere, the name it was generally known by until the
early 19th century.

John Dalton, the early 19th-century chemist and physicist
who developed the atomic theory of matter, grew up in

> With exultation at my feet, I saw
> Lake, islands, promontories, gleaming bays,
> A universe of Nature's fairest forms,
> Proudly reveal'd with instantaneous burst,
> Magnificent, and beautiful, and gay.

PLATE 4

SWAN INN, NEWBY BRIDGE, WINDERMERE

The Swan Hotel at Newby Bridge was originally a monastic farmhouse providing
beds for pilgrims to Furness Abbey and, after the Dissolution, became a coaching inn.

Newby Bridge.

Swan : *R.*, single, 4/–; double, 7/–
b., 2/6; *l.*, 2/6; *t.*, 1/–; *d.*, 5/–;
Boarding terms : 10/6 per day
73/6 per week; 21/– per weekend. Motor Garage.

Patterdale.

Ullswater.
Patterdale, Ullswater : *R.*, single, 2/–;
double, 3/–; *b.*, 2/–; *l.*, 2/–; *t.*
1/–; *d.*, 3/–; *a.*, 1/–.
Boarding terms : 7/6 per day;
52/6 per week; 15/– per weekend.
Milcrest's (*private*) : *R.*, single, fr.
2/–; double, 4/–; *b.*, 1/6; *l.*, 2/–;
t., 1/–; *d.*, 3/6.
Boarding terms on application.

The hamlet of Newby Bridge is in the Furness Peninsula, known as Lancashire North of the Sands until the administrative county boundary changes in 1974; it is now nominally in Cumbria. However, the local people still resist this and prefer to be known as the Lancastrians they feel they have always been. The region was somewhat cut off from the rest of Lancashire by its position above the treacherous sands of Morecambe Bay until the building of a turnpike road in 1763 linked it with Lonsdale. The Swan Hotel benefited from the new road and became an official stopping point for the Royal Mail stagecoach. The hotel's fine Georgian façade was added in 1766, and in 1782 the hotel was granted its first full licence. William Thomas Revell and his wife, the managers in 1906, were so convinced of its potential that they bought it 8 years later. Around this time the hotel and surrounding area were a hive of activity, thronged with coaches and the new "horseless carriages", together with the various cargoes being ferried either over the bridge or along the river.

NEWBY BRIDGE & SWAN HOTEL

PLATE 5

NEAR THE FERRY, WINDERMERE: SKATING BY MOONLIGHT

In some years Windermere freezes over completely; 1895, 1929, 1946 and 1963 each saw
a "great freeze", with skaters and ice yachters making the most of the polar conditions.

Skating by moonlight on a lake amidst snowy mountains must be a magical experience. Heaton Cooper would have experienced the "great freeze" of 1895, notable enough for the Victorian photographers to have risked life and equipment recording the event.

William Wordsworth was a skating aficionado, beginning on Esthwaite Water near Hawkshead in his schooldays. Canon Rawnsley's 1882 *Reminiscences of Wordsworth among the Peasantry of Westmorland* recounts how Grasmere folk knew Wordsworth as a "a ter'ble girt skater" (an extremely good skater).

All shod with steel
We hissed along the polished ice in games …
Not seldom from the uproar I retired
Into a silent bay …
To cut across the image of a star
That gleamed upon the ice.

William Wordsworth, *The Prelude*, 1798

In 1929, during the "great freeze", which later inspired his children's book Winter Holiday, Arthur Ransome was taught to skate on Windermere by the "saintly anarchist" Prince Kropotkin. The freezing over of Windermere is a vital part of the plot of the fourth Swallows and Amazons book.

PLATE 6

THE OLD FERRY, WINDERMERE

Between 1870 and 1915 a steam ferry ran from the
Claife side of Windermere to Ferry Nab in Bowness.

The Ferry Crossing   Windermere

The Windermere Ferry connects Bowness-on-Windermere with the villages of Far and Near Sawrey and Hawkshead, and there has been a ferry service at this point for centuries. The early ferries were rowing boats for which people called when they were in need of one; the steam-powered chain ferry shown in the postcard of 1905 was established by the Curwen family of nearby Belle Isle in 1870.

The Windermere Ferry is one of only 17 working chain ferries in Britain, the others being Bawdsey Ferry, Blyth High Ferry, Cowes Floating Bridge (Royal Ferry), Dartmouth Floating Bridge (Higher Ferry), Erskine Ferry, Portsmouth Floating Bridge (Gosport Ferry), Govan Ferry, King Harry Ferry, Reedham Ferry, Renfrew Ferry, Saltash Floating Bridge, Sandbanks Floating Bridge, Southwold Ferry, Torpoint Floating Bridge, Walney Ferry and Woolston Floating Bridge.

The wooded area on the west bank of the lake opposite Bowness, where there is also an old quarry, is known as Claife,

and is considered by many to be one of the most haunted places in the Lake District. The legend of the "Crier of Claife" was first recorded by the the writer and social critic Harriet Martineau, who had a house built for herself near Ambleside in 1845.

The legend relates that on wild and moonless nights a voice would call out "Boat! Boat!" from the Claife side. Most boatmen were wise enough to ignore it, but one wild and stormy night one of their number, either brave or foolhardy, chose to row over to answer the request. Half an hour later he returned with an empty boat, so terrified that he could not utter a word. His friends did their best for him but by the next morning he was dead.

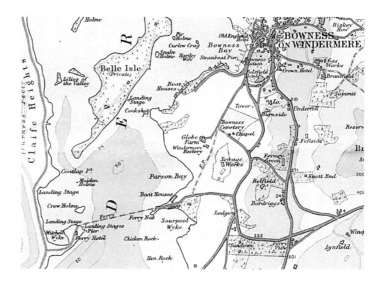

PLATE 7

OLD LABURNUMS AT NEWBY BRIDGE, WINDERMERE

A peaceful scene on the River Leven below Windermere at Newby Bridge,
the peacefulness affirmed by the presence of the gentle swan and the boat
waiting for its passenger.

The building could be part of the Newby Bridge Inn, and two figures, possibly children playing by the river – feeding the swan or dipping something in the water – are just visible in front of it. Or could they be an elderly couple taking a gentle stroll under the laburnums on this early summer day? The river is still and reflects the surroundings: trees, house and laburnums, though the reflections have less colour than the real trees which are bright and pretty when in full flower.

The laburnum is part of the pea family. There is also *Laburnum anagyroides* and, in Scotland, *Laburnum alpinum*. All parts of the laburnum tree are poisonous to humans, particularly the seeds, and the pea-like pods that gave the tree its former name of "peascod" were attractive to children so they were not planted in areas where children might play. The heartwood of laburnums is dark brown and very hard, and was sometimes used as a substitute for ebony before cabinet-makers knew about wood staining.

Laburnums were often planted in parks and gardens, popular because of their beautiful trailing bunches of flowers sometimes called "golden rain".

PLATE 8

WINDERMERE AND LANGDALE PIKES, FROM LOWWOOD

The Low Wood Hotel, formerly an inn, has been in this spot for nearly 300 years, and the panoramic view from the hotel has been an attraction for a number of famous visitors over those years.

Starting as a small farmstead, the Low Wood became an inn in the 1780s and, in 1782, became a posting house. Ten minutes were allowed for a change of horses and 30 minutes for a meal for passengers, indicating that the inn was a very busy place. Among its visitors were many famous artists, including Turner and Constable, all of whom came to paint one of the most classic views of the Langdale Pikes and accompanying hills. John Wright and his wife Mary were the innkeepers in 1793 – during the period which saw the birth of tourism in the Lake District. The Wrights would have benefited from the increasing number of visitors who travelled on the newly improved turnpike road which had reached Ambleside in 1761.

An eleven-year-old John Ruskin was enraptured by the view from his window on his first stay here. Nathaniel Hawthorne, a visitor from across the Atlantic, on a steamboat from Newby Bridge to Low Wood said "As we approached the head of the lake, the congregation of great hills in the distance became striking".

Between 1859 and the 1900s the inn, now an hotel, earned itself the reputation as a "honeymooners' hotel" with its private walks, lake sunsets over the Langdales and poetic associations, all being conducive to romantic thoughts.

PLATE 9

A GLIMPSE OF GRASMERE (EVENING SUN)

View of Grasmere from Loughrigg – in the distance is Dunmail Raise, the pass to northern Cumbria, its summit once the boundary line between Cumberland and Westmorland and, much earlier, the road to Scotland.

Thomas Gray, the famous poet and an early Lakes tourist, looked on Grasmere from Dunmail Raise in 1769 and what he saw pleased him mightily. After a detailed description of the lake and its surroundings he expresses himself happy that "not a single red tile, no gentleman's flaring house … break in upon the repose of this little unsuspected paradise". Some decades later, however, Wordsworth complained of the white houses, one in particular recently built that he could see from his cottage; white buildings, according to Wordsworth, being scars on the landscape. However, this did not prevent him inhabiting that house for some years before moving to Rydal.

The cairn on top of Dunmail Raise marks the spot where the British King Dunmail was supposedly killed in a battle he fought with King Malcolm of Scotland and the Saxon King Edmund in 945. The legend goes that King Dunmail's men built the cairn atop his body and threw his crown into Grisedale Tarn, high above, in the Helvellyn range. Whoever pulled it out would be next King of Cumbria.

Grasmere is known for annual sports, which include the traditional Lakeland activities of hound trails and the famous Cumberland and Westmorland wrestling. George Steadman was a legendary heavyweight wrestler whose last appearance at Grasmere Sports was in 1900, when he decided to give up on grounds of age. He died in 1904 aged 59.

WILD HYACINTHS

This scene is typical of the lower hills of Lakeland — wild hyacinth, primroses
and silver birches, with the rugged fells in the background.

Wild hyacinths, or bluebells (*Hyacinthoides non-scripta*), are part of the lily family, Liliaceae. In a recent poll conducted by the conservation group Plantlife they were voted the most popular of our wild flowers; as a result the bluebell was chosen as the wildflower emblem for the United Kingdom.

Today Britain has over half of the world's wild hyacinths. When this painting was completed, the bluebell could be seen carpeting woodlands (especially beech woods) and shady areas throughout the country. Now, however, this beautiful plant may be under threat. The problem is another member of the lily family, the Spanish bluebell (*Hyacinthoides hispanica*), which is a popular garden flower. The Spanish bluebell can cross breed with the native species and dilute its unique characteristics. Hybridisation alters a plant species' genetic makeup, and may result in a reduced ability to survive. A recent survey found that one in six broadleaved woodlands were found to contain either the Spanish bluebell or a hybrid.

Nowadays bluebells are a protected species, and taking them from the wild is illegal. However, in earlier times the bulbs were collected and their starch extracted and used for stiffening clothes. There was a superstition that bluebells could not be placed in a living room without dire consequences. Currently the bulbs are being investigated as potential treatments for cancer and HIV.

PLATE 11

DUNGEON GHYLL FORCE, LANGDALE

This waterfall, rugged and forbidding, drops alongside the popular route leading up the Langdale Pikes
and gave its name to the nearby Old Dungeon Ghyll Hotel in Great Langdale.

The name of England's famous historian, G.M. Trevelyan (1876–1962), is linked to this spot. In his youth he instituted a "man-hunt" with his friend Winthrop Young, a pioneer of British rock climbing and founder of the British Mountaineering Council. This event took place every Whitsuntide when a group of friends separated into "hounds" and "hares" and hunted each other around the central fells for three days. It continued until 1926. Trevelyan owned the building that became the old Dungeon Ghyll Hotel, formerly known as Middlefell Place, and in 1929 he gave it to the National Trust along with 50 acres of land. Thus it was that the National Trust came into possession of the historic buildings and farms at the head of Great Langdale and became a protector of the area before the creation of the National Park. This gave the landscape some degree of preservation from unsuitable and intrusive building. The name "force" comes from the Old Norse or Middle English word "fors", a waterfall; there are many such places in the Lake District where the mountain suddenly falls away leaving the water to drop from a great height in a single stream.

ALSO UNDER SAME MANAGEMENT.
LANGDALE VALLEY.

NEW HOTEL.
DUNGEON GHYLL.

The Hill Climbers' Paradise. In the heart of Lakeland Mountains.
The place for a restful holiday. Newly furnished throughout. Bathrooms.
Perfect Sanitary arrangements.

Routes via Windermere and Ambleside.

Telegraphic Address : "Elterwater."   J. COWPERTHWAITE,
Postal Address : "Ambleside."   Proprietor.

PLATE 12

DOVE COTTAGE, GRASMERE

Dove Cottage, Grasmere, is well known as the home of the poet,
William Wordsworth, who moved there in 1799 with his sister, Dorothy.
He married a few years later and their growing family lived at Dove Cottage until 1808.

The tiny cottage, formerly an inn called The Dove and Olive Branch, is unbelievably small for the number of people who were occasionally quartered there. The front porch leads into the houseplace, where, in Wordsworth's time, most of the "living" took place. This room is not only minuscule in dimensions, it is also low-ceilinged, so tall people would have needed to take care. Some upstairs rooms are even more restricted. All the more surprising therefore that the cottage was a temporary home to several literary figures as well as the family that inhabited it. Coleridge spent long periods there and Walter Scott was a visitor, as were Thomas De Quincey, Charles and Mary Lamb, Robert Southey and William Hazlitt. The Wordsworths lived very simply, to the extent, so it is told, that Scott used to sneak up to the local inn to get a good meal.

The Wordsworth Trust took over Dove Cottage and named it so in 1891. The Trust has taken care to preserve the garden as it was as far as possible, and to continue growing the plants that were there originally. These include wild myrtle, grass of Parnassus, red and white dead nettle and, of course, wild daffodils (*Narcissus pseudonarcissus*, not the cultivated kind that is now planted in Lakeland), as well as trees such as rowan and hazel.

PLATE 13

SKELWITH FORCE, LANGDALE

These beautiful, turbulent falls on the River Brathay at the hamlet of Skelwith Bridge
have long been a fascination for visitors like this lady sitting on the rocks.

At this point the wide river is constrained between rocks that create a tumbling heap of bubbling water which slides down the slope into the whirlpool below. This is a dangerous place to try and swim, though at times of low water a swim in the pool is possible for the more adventurous – or foolhardy. The Langdale Pikes can be glimpsed in the distance, a view that the growing trees have now obscured.

Just below the falls there have been several industries. Jeremiah Coward used to run the Skelwith Bridge Saw Mills, making bobbins for the Lancashire cotton mills. Another well-known bobbin factory in the Lake District was the Stott Park Bobbin Mill, at Finsthwaite on the road between Newby Bridge and Hawkshead. This closed in 1971 and is now a museum. Prior to 1905 the area by the river at Skelwith was used for the storage and drying of wood in the production of gunpowder. Today, Kirkstone Quarries produce slate for roofs, flooring, cladding and other building work, which is exported all over the world.

PLATE 14

SUNSET, RYDAL WATER

This view is of Rydal Water, the lake lying next to Grasmere,
and of the River Rothay. Yellow gorse and foxgloves are prominent in the foreground.

The level of the water here, covering the shoreline in parts, indicates that the weather has recently been rainy, not unusual in the Lake District. This is a peaceful scene with grazing sheep, a smooth, still lake, and an island of trees lying in the middle of the water.

Today this view, from White Moss Common, is completely obscured by trees and vegetation. The meadows are now wetland filled with tall rushes. The location is close to the house, Rydal Mount, where William Wordsworth and his family lived from 1813 until his death in 1850, and the small church at Rydal that the family attended. On the road running beside Rydal Water is Nab Cottage where Hartley Coleridge, son of Samuel Taylor Coleridge, lived the last years of his life as a lodger to the Richardson family; he died here in 1849. During these last years Hartley Coleridge was a well-known and popular presence around the two villages. He was a man of intellectual promise never fulfilled owing to his dependence on alcohol, who, nevertheless, became a favourite character in the area and was particularly cared for by the Wordsworths.

Gorse is a common flowering shrub in the Lake District, and it is said that the 18th-century botanist Carl Linnaeus fell on his knees and wept at the sight of English gorse in all its glory. It did not grow in his native Sweden.

PLATE 15

GRASMERE CHURCH

The pretty squat-towered church of St Oswald in Grasmere, dating from the 14th century,
stands in a large churchyard bordered on two sides by the winding River Rothay.

The graves of William Wordsworth, his immediate family and Hartley Coleridge are in the churchyard near the river, and there is a memorial to Wordsworth in the church.

In 1500 an extra nave was built onto the church, called the Langdale Aisle. Grasmere Church is famous for its Rushbearing Festival traditionally held every year on the Saturday nearest to St Oswald's Day (6 August), when children walk in procession through the village carrying their "bearings", decorations of various appropriate kinds made with rushes. They process to the church where a Service of Thanksgiving takes place, leave their bearings around the church, and then receive a traditional award of gingerbread stamped with the name of St Oswald. The custom is said to have derived from the fact that the floor of the church was of flattened earth until the mid-19th century, with people buried underneath it, and so rushes were a necessary air-purifier. There are several recognised fiddle tunes and a march associated with the Rushbearing Festival — the earliest known fiddler was Jimmy Dawson. The Wordsworths and De Quincey had all walked in the processions. A painting of the Rushbearing by Frank Bramley RA, local to Grasmere and whose memorial tablet is in the church, was exhibited at the Royal Academy in 1905 and purchased by public subscription for the village in 1913.

10017. - GRASMERE CHURCH.

PLATE 16

ESTHWAITE WATER: APPLE BLOSSOM

Esthwaite Water is a small lake set amidst meadows and rolling green
countryside south of Hawkshead, between the lakes of Windermere and Coniston.

Low-lying as it is, Esthwaite has a particularly rich flora. Here are trees bedecked with apple blossom and surrounded by a carpet of wild daffodils. The lake is 2.5 km long and 600 metres wide, and the cattle indicate that the land around was farmed then much as it is today.

Anglers keen to cast a line whilst visiting the Lake District will be delighted by the diversity of fishing available in and around the Hawkshead area. Esthwaite Water rates as one of the finest fishing waters in the Lake District. Predominantly a trout fishery, Esthwaite Water also boasts both excellent pike and coarse fishing. Other fish found there include rudd, roach and trout. Birds such as osprey and great crested grebe can still be seen today.

The lake is near Colthouse, a group of houses and other buildings that include a Quaker Meeting House. Beatrix Potter, who later married a local solicitor, is known to have attended a Quaker Meeting there in 1896. The cottage she lived in for many years is nearby at Hill Top, Near Sawrey. At the northern end of Hawkshead village, on the road to Ambleside, is the Old Hall, a building once owned by the monks of Furness who lived there while they were collecting their tithes.

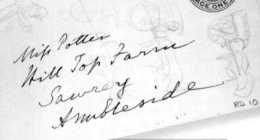

PLATE 17

AN OLD STREET IN HAWKSHEAD

One of several, fascinating, crooked little streets in this quaint and
pretty town at the northern end of Esthwaite Water.

The buildings and streets in this tiny town were often designed
to suit their particular purpose, as in the "overhanging pentices"
that provided cover for the wool and cloth stalls on market days.
Wordsworth Street was once called Leather, Rag and Putty
Street, reflecting the trades carried on in it. Thimble Hall was
purportedly so named because a seamstress and her leatherworker
husband lived and worked there. Grandy Nook (Grandmother's
Corner) is situated where the lane divides and one part goes
under an archway beneath cottages, that lane having been a
packhorse route to the Furness Peninsula. In order to enable
the horse and cart to turn, a small open area was left among the
cottages. William Wordsworth attended the grammar school
in Hawkshead, which was built in 1785 by Archbishop Edwin
Sandys, whose descendants still live in the area. There is a
memorial to him in the church, probably the first building you
see when approaching Hawkshead from the south, standing high
up on a small hill. An interesting exhibit, now in the Queen's
Hotel, is Haaksids Girt Clog
(Hawkshead's Great Clog).
This shoe – 51 cm long, 20 cm
wide across the bottom, and
40 cm across the front, with
an 18 cm heel – was made for
a man with elephantiasis in
his left foot.

PLATE 18

SHEEP-SHEARING, ESTHWAITE HALL FARM

This barn, dateable to 1520, is a fine example of a cruck barn, and is now being restored
as far as possible to its original state by the Sandys family of nearby Graythwaite Hall.

At the time of this painting, sheep were often sheared by visiting gangs of sheep-shearers or farms would get together to help each other. This gave rise to the custom of "boon" days when everyone mucked in to help and was rewarded with food, drink and music.

The sheep in this picture will have had to be counted – the systems of counting were ancient and varied from region to region. In Cumberland the words used for the numbers from one to ten were yan, tyan, tethera, methera, pimp, sethera, lethera, hovera, dovra, dick.

These are probably Rough Fell sheep, which have white faces, rather than Herdwick, which are darker and have rougher fleeces, not as suitable for dyeing. Herdwicks, however, are very hardy and nimble on the rocky fells. The *Westmorland Gazette* of 29 April 1905 states: "Strayed to Graythwaite Hall Home Farm two months since, an old Herdwick Ewe marked red over loins, underbitten in near ear". This indicates the ownership markings on that particular sheep, the red colouring rubbed into the fleece and the ear clipped in a special way. It is interesting because Herdwick rarely stray, having a homing instinct which ensures they remember for life the "heaf" where they first grazed.

PLATE 19

DAWN, CONISTON

A beautiful picture of rosy dawn on the fells behind Coniston seen from the lake shore.
Early morning mist rises from the waters round the figure rowing his boat.

Various origins are given for the name of Coniston, among them "Conyngestun" from *c.*1160, meaning "King's town" in Old Norse. An earlier name for Coniston was Thorstein, and there is a novel, written in 1895 by John Ruskin's secretary, W.G. Collingwood, called *Thorstein of the Mere*, the story of the Norse settler who gave the lake its ancient name.

A story told about Coniston is that Arthur Ransome's father once dropped him in the lake when he was a young child, to see if, like some animals, he could swim naturally. He couldn't, but fortunately his father saved him and he lived to tell the tale – or tales in Arthur Ransome's case. The experience obviously gave the young Arthur a taste for Coniston Water because he later learned to row on it and, of course, some of his best children's stories are set on this lake.

Those fells, here copper-coloured by the morning sun, have also contained large amounts of copper. Mining began here in Elizabethan times when that valuable substance was found 1600 feet down on Coniston Old Man. German miners were brought over, being experts in this field, and consequently settled in the area. Slate was also mined, and the quarries can still be seen, as can the streets of terraced houses for the miners, looking rather incongruous in a Lakeland landscape.

PLATE 20

CHARCOAL-BURNERS, CONISTON LAKE

Charcoal-burners, one of Heaton Cooper's favourite subjects, go about their business
at the southern end of Coniston Lake. Coniston Old Man is in the distance.

The tree in the foreground is a silver birch and the distant view is of hills at the head of the lake. Coppiced wood lies around ready for burning to make charcoal. According to records, it is probable that the Furness monks began the business of manufacturing charcoal and taking wood from around "Thurstainwater" across the lake to Furness. The industry was probably carried on by others after the dissolution of Furness Abbey in 1537, once mining became locally established.

The charcoal industry became extremely important from the 16th century onwards in southern Lakeland, for the smelting activities of the Mines Royal Company. It was also useful for the manufacture of gunpowder. In the 18th century charcoal was one of the main cargoes carried on Coniston. The makers of charcoal had to spend six or seven days at a time living in the woods while the charcoal was forming because it needed constant attention. They used to make themselves temporary bivouacs out of whatever materials were available.

Charcoal burners were always welcome because they kept the forest clear of dead wood, and the coppicing helped regenerate trees such as alder, birch, beech and juniper.

PLATE 21

BRANTWOOD, CONISTON LAKE: CHAR-FISHING

Brantwood was the home of John Ruskin, from 1872 until his death in 1900, and now is open to the public.
Char-fishing was popular on several lakes in Lakeland, including Coniston.

Coniston is associated with several famous names. John Ruskin, philanthropist and art historian, bought Brantwood in 1872 from William Linton. Linton himself (1812–98) was a skilled wood-engraver and political reformer who lived there from 1852 to 1872 and later married the novelist and journalist, Eliza Lynn (1822–98). The house is now a memorial, mainly to Ruskin but also to Linton (a showcase is devoted to him). Ruskin made additions to the property, notably the turret room with windows all round, providing a wider view of Coniston lake and the imposing array of hills opposite. It was this view that induced Ruskin to buy the house in the first place.

Char-fishing was popular as far back as the early 18th century. After the glacial waters of the last Ice Age receded, the arctic char became landlocked in Coniston, Bassenthwaite, Derwentwater and Windermere. Related to salmon, char taste like a delicate version of sea trout, and are popular potted or in pies. They are still caught on the lake today, in season from July to October. The most successful method of catching char is by trailing bright metal spinners on long lines deep into the water. Char fishermen row along the lake to keep the lures moving continually.

Arthur Ransome first visited the Lake District in 1891, staying at Nibthwaite south of the lake. He set his novel *Swallows and Amazons* in the area.

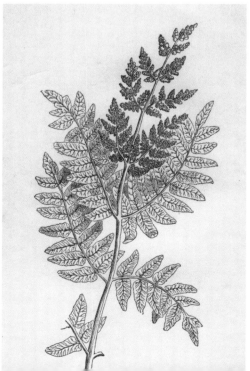

PLATE 22

CONISTON VILLAGE:
THE OLD BUTCHER'S SHOP

A view of Yewdale Crags beyond the butcher's shop,
a row of cottages, and the Black Bull Inn.

These cottages have the distinctive chimney types that are found everywhere on old cottages in the Lake District. The houses are on a hill, showing how the slope affects the house floor levels and the cottages' relationship to each other. They have since been made into comfortable modern residences. The Black Bull Inn, a large, comfortable 16th-century inn, most likely a coaching inn at one time, can be seen in the background. Just opposite the cottages, off the picture on the right, is St Andrew's Church, built in 1891, and the large churchyard where John Ruskin's is buried. W.G. Collingwood, a writer and private secretary to John Ruskin for a time, made an entertaining recreation of the life of a 17th-century curate of this church in a novel, *Dutch Agnes Her Valentine*, published in 1910.

In terms of the meat available to local butchers, the Lake District is mainly sheep-farming country, because sheep are versatile and nimble enough to live in the rough, fell landscape, but cattle are also farmed on the lower-lying areas. In the past most families kept a pig, and the butcher might be called in to assist at the annual pig-killing day which required plenty of skill to produce sausages, black puddings, hams, bacon and pork.

PLATE 23

MOONLIGHT AND LAMPLIGHT, CONISTON

An early winter evening view, with a bright moon and
welcoming lamplight glowing in the cottage window.

This picture was reviewed by the art critic of the *Westmorland Gazette* of 12 August 1905 as one of several "delicate experiments to attempt to express admiration of the Lake District in this way, and it has succeeded beyond what could have been hoped". Light is coming from the moon, the white house and the lamplit window. The prowling cat is watching out for any adventurous mice.

Another house in Coniston, interesting because of those who have lived there, is Tent Lodge on the lake shore. where a learned young woman called Elizabeth Smith lived from 1801 to 1806. She studied German, Spanish, French, Italian, Greek, Hebrew, Arabic and some Persian languages, and was self-taught in all except French, to the point of being able to translate the Book of Job in the Old Testament from Hebrew.

Unfortunately Elizabeth's health was poor and she slept in a tent on the lawn because of her consumptive condition, dying at the age of 29. Other residents of Tent Lodge, however briefly, have been the poet, Alfred Lord Tennyson and Arthur Ransome.

PLATE 24

AN OLD INN KITCHEN, CONISTON

This scene is of an old kitchen, which dates back to at least the 18th century, with a spice cupboard
in the background, huge plates on the rack and a bunch of onions on the wall.

The stone-flagged inn kitchen has thick wooden beams holding up the roof, a huge fireplace and a cooking range. The cat is a useful resident for a place where there are, no doubt, many mice. The table is set for a beer drinker, with a huge hunk of bread and cheese – simple food. The door is wide and appears too low for a tall person to pass through without stooping. The sad-looking woman may be in mourning, dressed in black as she is. Could the young woman be a neighbour or a companion, or could they both be employees of the inn, during a quiet time? The inn is the Ship Inn, Bowmanstead, Coniston, on the road to Torver.

Char would be a regular dish offered in inns around here, being obtained from Lake Coniston. Potted char was a Lakeland delicacy, and each inn had a stew, a container for keeping the char in until they were ready to be cooked. *West's Guide* mentions one Coniston inn with a well-filled stew. Char pie was another favourite dish in the 18th century.

PLATE 25

THE SHEPHERD, YEWDALE, CONISTON

A shepherd and his dog sitting among the higher hills around Coniston,
waterfalls tumbling down the hill and rain misting the hilltops.

These are the Yewdale Fells at the north-western end of Coniston Water, towering over the village. Waterfalls in plenty flow down these fellsides, fluctuating in size and shape according to the weather. Hill sheep farming came with the Norsemen, but did not begin to flourish fully here until the wolf population was wiped out in the 15th century – placenames like Uldale imply that wolves were once in the area. The traditional Cumbrian sheep breed is the Herdwick, the name itself meaning "sheep farm", and it is thought the Norsemen brought these sheep with them. Herdwick are "terrible lish", that is, very agile, and the ewes are without horns. A tradition is that the sheep go with the farm and are taken over when a farm is sold. This may be because the sheep become accustomed to a "heaf", an area from which they will not stray even though there are no physical boundaries to it.

There is a famous farm called High Yewtree Farm near Coniston, recently in the news because it has been sold by the National Trust and broken up among several new owners. Yewtree Farm has a "spinning gallery", a gallery attached to the front of the second storey, often on the north or east wall, where housewives would sit of an evening and spin sheep's wool, making the most of the available daylight.

PLATE 26

STEPPING-STONES, SEATHWAITE

Seathwaite stepping-stones cross the River Duddon between
Wallowbarrow Crag on the left and Hollin Tongue on the right.

Seathwaite is a hamlet with a church, the Newfield Inn, and a few houses. In the 18th century the church had a curate called Robert Walker, who remained in the post for 66 years. He was known as "Wonderful Walker", not a reference to his fell-walking prowess, but to the fact that he was considered a saintly, good and generous man and was very popular in his small parish. He lived very simply and added to his income by farm work such as sheep clipping, and by teaching in the village school. He was born in the hamlet and his grave is in the churchyard. He left a small fortune – £2000 – amassed from all his little extra jobs.

The Seathwaite stepping-stones are the subject of two of Wordsworth's Duddon Sonnets, where he says of them:

Stone matched for stone
In studied symmetry, with interspace
For the clear waters to pursue their race
Without restraint.

Seathwaite had a reputation in the late 19th century for good sheep-shearing, and a visitor walking through Seathwaite in 1890 described exactly how he saw it done, from the way the sheep is held, to the fleece coming off in one piece and the naked sheep escaping.

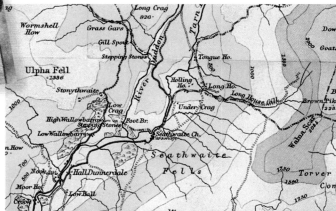

PLATE 27

WINTER SUNSHINE, CONISTON

A view of a fine house in Coniston with Coniston Old Man rearing up behind,
and a farmer taking a stack of hay into his barn to feed his animals indoors.

This is truly a winter scene, with snow on the lower ground as well as on the high fells. Snowy landscapes among hills are beautiful, particularly on a moonlit night, but snow could be a problem for sheep farmers in the Lake District in the days when snowfalls were heavier than they are now. There were several winters when the lakes froze over solid enough to walk about on; lakes became thoroughfares and people drove cars and carriages on the ice. But sheep could become snowbound, get buried under drifts and die there. Farmers had to go out with their dogs to sniff them out and rescue them. Sometimes it could be a hazardous task because the sheep had fallen into almost inaccessible places, which were dangerous for a person to attempt – this is where the shepherd's crook was an essential piece of equipment. However, the skilful, nimble dogs could usually manage at least to locate them, though the retrieving might be more difficult. In such weather farmers always risk losing some sheep, even though the sheep know instinctively when snow is approaching and tend to make for the shelter of drystone walls. Sheep have been known to survive for several weeks under the snow.

PLATE 28

DAFFODILS BY THE BANKS
OF THE SILVERY DUDDON

The River Duddon rises in the high fells around Wrynose and hugs the Wrynose Pass and
Wrynose Bottom before the valley widens as the river progresses to the sea.

The Duddon Valley is long and varied in its landscape, the highest reaches being lonely and wild, the lower well populated with farms and villages. Wordsworth was very fond of the Duddon Valley. He describes it in his *Guide to the Lakes* thus: "the vale of Duddon, in which is no lake but a copious stream winding among fields, rocks and mountains and terminating its course in the sands of the Duddon."

A Roman road has been traced crossing the River Duddon at Wrynose Bottom and continuing on its northern bank for a mile or so before branching off.

In the 12th century the River Duddon was the boundary of a disputed area, the dispute being between one of the most extensive landowners in Lakeland, Furness Abbey, and William de Lancaster, Baron of Kendal. It was resolved by a committee of men whose names — Ulf, Ketel, Swein — indicate their Scandinavian origins.

There is a story told that some students in the 19th century who were staying at the public house at Ulpha in the Duddon Valley decided to test the landlord by asking for their bill in Latin. The landlord, being a well-educated man, replied in Greek, which floored the students.

PLATE 29

A FELL FOX-HUNT, HEAD OF ESKDALE AND SCAWFELL

A fox-hunt is in full cry at the head of the Eskdale Valley,
with the great peaks of the Scafell range behind.

Fox-hunting in the Lake District was done on foot rather than on horseback, as the terrain is far too rough for horses. It was not thought of as a sport, as in many parts of England, but as a necessity to protect sheep, lambs and other livestock.

The Eskdale and Ennerdale Farmers' Hunt was founded in 1857 by Tommy Dobson, a bobbin turner and legendary huntsman in this area. Huntsmen such as Tommy were country heroes – his tombstone at St Catherine's Church has a carving of his face as well as the heads of both a hound and a fox. He died in 1910. Though not a locally born man, coming from South Westmorland, he settled in Eskdale and built up a good pack of hounds.

Hardknott Pass, a difficult and hair-raising road to negotiate, being a series of extremely steep hairpin bends, leads into the head of Eskdale. On top of this pass lies the remains of a Roman fort, still visible, with low walls, commanding a flat area that overlooks the dale.

PLATE 30

WASTWATER, FROM STRANDS

Strands is the area at the lower end of Wastwater.
This view is looking up the lake towards the famous peaks of Great Gable and Scafell.

Strands, or Nether Wasdale, has one public house, once a temperance inn, and a few other buildings. The countryside around is comparatively gentle compared with that of the mountain range at the lake's top end. Coleridge called at this inn for a "dish of tea" on his way to Wasdale Head to start his well-reported climb and dangerous descent. The inn in those times would have been a large stone-floored room, comparatively bare, though in winter there would have been a comforting fire in the large hearth. On the right of this view can be seen the beginnings of the screes, slopes of loose stones falling 183 metres sheer into the lake.

Boats on the lake always look dwarfed by their majestic surroundings. It must be tempting to sail near the screes to experience the feeling that the entire mountain might be falling down on top of you. Perhaps that is the experience the Edwardians had, tourists having by then overcome the fear of the hills that was common among visitors a hundred years earlier. Wastwater has been described as "the most Scandinavian of the lakes", and it is, both in appearance and wildness and in the types of remains left by the Norse settlers, who obviously favoured this place because it so resembled their homeland.

G. P. Abraham.] THE HEAD OF WASTWATER AND GREAT GABLE, [Keswick.

PLATE 31

WASTWATER AND SCAWFELL

Scawfell, now known as Scafell, stands 978 metres in all its majesty at the head of Wastwater.

Wastwater sits in the valley of Wasdale, considered the birthplace of British climbing. The Wasdale Head Inn is one of the most famous in Lakeland for various reasons, not least because it has been used as a base for rock climbers since the 1880s. Among the first Lakeland rock-climbing pioneers were young undergraduates from Oxford and Cambridge who spent a "reading week" in the area in the 1880s and whose rock-climbing exploits, using the most basic of equipment, helped to establish the new sport of climbing. Walter Parry Haskett-Smith, a legendary figure in rock climbing, is of this period and his books on the subject were enormously influential. There are climbers' graves in St Olaf's churchyard in Wasdale.

Alfred Wainwright, a well-known 20th-century author of several books about the Lake District, waxes lyrical and philosophises about climbing when talking about Scafell Pike. He describes people's apparent need to climb mountains and the satisfaction they derive and, in contrasting mood, he describes the impact of visitors on the summit: "Man's contribution to the scene is a huge circular platform ... a plaque ... and litter. There is no beauty here."

A comment from the visitors' book of a local inn on 11 November 1905 read: "Scawfell is awfell, Rossett Ghyll makes you ill"; obviously not a good experience for this particular party.

This view of Scafell from Wastwater is a magical one of untamed, almost untouched, nature.

PLATE 32

WASTDALEHEAD AND GREAT GABLE (TOWARDS EVENING IN AUTUMN)

Wasdale Head (the modern spelling) is at the northern end of Wastwater,
a valley surrounded by two of the highest hills in Lakeland, Scafell and Great Gable.

This view looks up the valley to the peak of Great Gable. Moses Trod is the path that leads to this fell, named supposedly after a quarryman who made illicit whisky at his quarry hut and smuggled it into Wasdale among his loads of slate.

Great Gable is 899 metres high and, viewed from Wasdale Head, appears like the gable end of a huge church; it includes the terrifying Napes Needle which the famous rock climber, Walter Parry Haskett-Smith, climbed in 1886.

On the top of Great Gable there is a bronze war memorial and, every Remembrance Sunday, as many as a hundred walkers climb to the top to observe the two minutes' silence there. The summit of Great Gable, and much land surrounding it, was purchased by the Fell and Rock Climbing Club and presented to the National Trust in 1924 in memory of the Club's 20 members who were killed in World War I. It is to them that the war memorial is dedicated.

Joss Naylor is a retired shepherd and legendary fell runner who still lives in Wasdale. One of his greatest records was to run up 61 summits, a total of 90 miles, in 24 hours, with a climb of 34,000 feet (10,363 metres).

Another famous name associated with the area is Hugh Walpole, the novelist, whose clergyman father took a living at Gosforth, west of Wastwater, in 1893 when Hugh was a child. This enabled him to explore the area, staying at Sower Myre Farm, climbing Great Gable, and picnicking by Wastwater. The writer Lewis Carroll was also a frequent visitor to the area in the 1890s, having relatives at Holmrook Hall.

PLATE 33

WASTWATER SCREES

In the English Lake District screes such as this are unique to Wastwater;
it is said that these slopes plunge as far below the water as they stretch above it.

The screes are the first things that draw the eye when arriving at the lower end of Wastwater. They are compelling and bewitching because, from the safety of the opposite shore, it is amazing that people can be seen actually walking along a path a little way up among these apparently falling stones. The word "scree" probably comes from the Norse word "skritha", meaning landslide, and it is difficult to believe that the slightest mis-step would not start an avalanche that could send someone plunging into the lake, or worse. A safer way to look at them, while still feeling a little thrill of danger, is from a boat on the lake close to the southern shore.

The most impressive views are when the lake is still and the hills are reflected in it. Coleridge describes this in a letter to Sara Hutchinson: "and all this reflected, turned in Pillars and a whole new-world of Images, in the water".

Wastwater is said to be the deepest lake in England. However, not even the deepest lake could conceal forever the remains of Margaret Hogg, whose body was dumped in the lake by her husband and discovered by divers in 1985 while searching for a missing French tourist, who was later found dead on the screes.

PLATE 34

WASTDALEHEAD CHURCH

This tiny church in Wasdale Head, dedicated to St Olaf, is said to be
the smallest in England, though there may be some challengers to this.

Wasdale Head Church was dedicated to St Olaf in 1977, though the present building dates from the 18th century, and the site is more ancient than that. The churchyard was consecrated in 1901. It is surrounded by yew trees, which can safely be planted in churchyards because yews are poisonous to feeding stock. Churches or chapels were built in areas such as this in the 16th century to provide spiritual sustenance for the people who were starting to make their living there. Owing to its position near rock-climbing crags, there are many climbers buried in the churchyard who have come to grief nearby. The Fell and Rock Climbing Club also has a moving memorial window to those of its members who were killed in World War I. The window has a diamond-shaped stained glass image of Napes Needle with the immortal words "I will lift up mine eyes unto the hills … "

Some historic links refer to Olaf as a martyred King of Norway, others say that he was a Norwegian soldier who died in battle here in 1030. There is a local tradition that the ancient rafters were once the timbers of a Viking ship.

PLATE 35

NEARING THE TOP OF
STYHEAD PASS, WASTDALE

Great End and the narrow track for walkers up this col would surely have terrified many early tourists;
Thomas Gray, the famous 18th-century poet, carefully avoided using it.

Wasdale is linked to Borrowdale, for walkers, by the narrow Sty Head Pass, which begins at Stockley Bridge, Borrowdale. This view from the top shows the impressive bulk of Great End. The path leads down into the hamlet of Wasdale, which was at the height of its fame as a British rock climbing centre from the end of the 19th century, reaching its peak in 1910.

The Wasdale Head Inn (formerly the "Huntsmans' Inn" belonging to Will Ritson, a well-known 18th-century farmer, huntsman and wrestler) became famous as the hotel for rock climbers. Traditional events there also included Shepherd's Meets and "murry neets" (Merry Nights). Easter was an especially popular time for the climbing fraternity to visit Wasdale, to the point that there were often not enough beds, and guests had to sleep on tops of billiard tables and even in baths! High cuisine was not a speciality for this clientele and has been described as "stewed frayed rope and rice pudding", but there was plenty of it and the emphasis everywhere was on informality. It was noted that the few ladies who stayed there at the turn of the century had difficulty preserving the niceties.

Famous cragsmen of the time included Walter Parry Haskett-Smith, Owen Glynne Jones, and the Abraham Brothers, George and Ashley, who were climbers and also had a photography business in Keswick.

A popular entertainment at country fairs used to be, and still is, that of "gurning" (grinning), in which shepherds compete in making the ugliest face, framing their faces in a horse collar. A man called Owd Joe apparently won it without even trying, just by expressing facial interest during a conversation.

PLATE 36

WASTDALEHEAD, WASTWATER

Wastdale Head with its group of farm buildings and packhorse bridge
on a cloudy day with the hills scarcely visible.

A well-known name in Wastdale was Will Ritson, a farmer in Wastdalehead born in 1808, keen huntsman and wrestler. He met the rich, young John Wilson (Christopher North of the famous Victorian literary publication, *Blackwood's Magazine*) who was visiting Wastdale for the sport. A very keen sportsman, Wilson introduced other people to the valley. Will Ritson became an interest for those in the Lakeland literary scene, as he was famous for his repartee and tall stories; so many people came to his farmhouse that he decided to rename it the Huntsmans' Inn and to license it.

This area was also an attraction for keen rock and hill climbers who flocked to this isolated valley. From the early 1880s onwards, mountaineers and hill walkers were developing an interest in rock climbing and starting to use their hands as well as their feet for progressing. Among the keen climbers of this time was Sir Leslie Stephen (1832–1904), father of the writer Virginia Woolf.

The first woman to climb the challenging Pillar Rock was Miss A. Barker in 1870. Another great climber of that time was a clergyman called James Jackson (nicknamed "Steeple Jackson" because he climbed the steeple of his own church). Born in 1796, James Jackson started climbing in later life and was still climbing in his 80s. He died on the fells in snow in 1878.

There is now an annual Biggest Liars' Competition at Santon Bridge, formerly held at Wastdale, Will Ritson's home, where people try to outdo each other by telling tall stories and hoping to be believed.

ENNERDALE LAKE AT SUNSET

Ennerdale is one of the more inaccessible lakes in the Lake District
with no villages around it and no public vehicle access through the valley.

Ennerdale is the most westerly of the lakes, impossible to approach by road except from the west. The valley is eight miles long, and because of its comparative isolation was targeted by the Forestry Commission in the 1920s and covered with conifers in serried rows. Two thousand sheep were expelled from their grazing areas. Now the lines have been softened but this is still the valley with the most rugged pass, Black Sail. The Black Sail Hostel is much appreciated for the loneliness of its location by the many walkers and climbers who use it.

In 1883 there was a plan to run a railway through the pass. Canon Rawnsley, ever dependable as the saviour of Lakeland, opposed it along with the Lake District Defence Society, and it did not happen, but the *Pall Mall Gazette* published a poem on it:

> Wake, England, wake! Tis, now the hour
> To sweep away this black disgrace
> The want of locomotive power
> In so enjoyable a place.
> Nature has done her part and why
> Is mightier man in his to fail?
> I want to hear the porter's cry
> "Change here for Ennerdale!"

Ennerdale's romantic fastnesses also aided smugglers; Moses Trod, a path named after an illicit whisky distiller, was used to reach Borrowdale by way of Great Gable and thus evade the excise men.

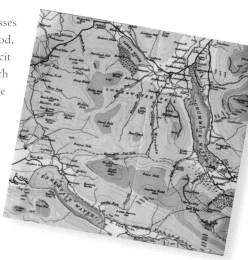

PLATE 38

THE PILLAR ROCK OF ENNERDALE

Pillar Rock dominates the south-west Pillar group of fells and is 892 metres high,
sheer, and a challenge to would-be climbers.

This area has always attracted climbers, and Wainwright admits that it could be "a place of horror, awful and ugly", at least to the timid observer. Walter Parry Haskett-Smith, the legendary 19th-century rock climber, climbed Pillar Rock in 1891.

In the *Westmorland Gazette* of 24 June 1905 can be found: "Attempts have been made recently by various skilful cragsmen to effect an ascent of Pillar Rock at its north-west corner … It has several times been attacked at this point … On that day a party of climbers staying at the Wastwater Hotel volunteered to wait on the summit of Low Man with ropes, in case help should be needed."

John Wilson Robinson, a well-known early climber, died there in 1907, and has a memorial on what is now called Robinson's Cairn. It has a plaque reading:

> We climb the hill from end to end
> In all the landscape underneath;
> We find no place that does not breathe
> Some gracious memory of our friend.

Climbing gear in 1905 was primitive by modern standards, and was often little more than normal daily wear, slightly adapted to cope with the weather. Without the garments we have today to keep out the soaking rain and the strong boots to cope with hard and rocky surfaces, the achievement of these early rock climbers is all the more admirable.

PLATE 39

LOWESWATER

Loweswater is a small lake, a mile north-west of Crummock Water in flat fields within Lorton Vale.
Surrounding it are the fells of Grasmoor, Whiteside and Mellbreak, after which the Mellbreak Hunt is named.

Wordsworth wrote a poem about the yew tree known as the "Pride of Lorton Vale". It is over a thousand years old and still standing. Both George Fox, founder of the Society of Friends or Quakers, and John Wesley, founder of Methodism, are said to have preached under it.

Doreen Wallace, born in 1897, the daughter of the founder of the well-known Wallace Collection of Art in London, was a novelist who spent 15 years of her childhood in Lorton. There is a story that she once protected a fox seeking shelter from the Mellbreak Hunt in a greenhouse on her land until the hunt had gone away.

As in many sheep-farming communities, sheep dipping takes place here regularly, running sheep through a liquid disinfectant to protect them from disease. In 1905 the older and far more labour-intensive method of salving was usually employed. The whole flock had to be individually salved – all of the wool of each sheep down to the skin had to be rubbed by hand with a mixture of grease and tar against the scourge of "scab".

PLATE 40

THE OLD POST OFFICE, LOWESWATER

Loweswater is a tiny secluded lake with a few farms, north-west of Crummock Water,
and this old farm was obviously used as the local post office.

At the turn of the 19th century post offices in remote areas like this would have been run by local people taking on various jobs, including postal delivery, that often involved a good knowledge of the district and much walking. Before World War I, post offices were open for business and telegraph messages from 8 a.m. to 8 p.m., but during the war, and after, hours were much reduced.

The people who delivered the letters were at first known as messengers, only later as postmen or women, and had long daily walks, often having to leave letters in boxes at lane ends, from which they also collected, because postboxes were rare in these country areas. Postal services were very good, and even heavy snow failed to deter the postmen from walking their rounds.

The post office would have had one of the few telephones in the village, and a telegram service that depended on casual labour for deliveries. In some cases, children were employed to do this. It was often the case that post offices were set up in a general shop in the village, as they still are. From the picture it appears that a suitable location for a post office had been found on this farmstead.

Roland Hill, who introduced the penny post, also initiated a late afternoon mail collection in Ambleside to accommodate local writer Harriet Martineau, so that manuscripts could reach her editors early next morning in London. In those days people wrote postcards much as we now use the telephone or email, to arrange meetings or exchange an observation. In 1912 the Post Office introduced a national telephone service.

PLATE 41

CRUMMOCK WATER, FROM SCALE HILL

Crummock Water seen from Scale Hill with a view of Melbreak
and the Buttermere Fells, cloud-capped and indistinct.

This painting depicts the kind of terrain used for hound trailing, a popular sport in many parts of Lakeland. An autumn scene shows a few brown-leafed silver birches among the bracken and brush with heather on the bank among the pine trees.

As in 1905, hound trailing still takes place today from April to October, and is particularly associated with country agricultural shows. Just before the race, a trail of paraffin and aniseed is laid over the fells for several miles then, when the race is due to start, the owners stand in a long row with their dogs, ready to release them at the off whistle. The expectant dogs are hysterical with excitement, yelping and crying until they are "slipped", and race off at full speed. Even more exciting and dramatic is the end of a hound trail when owners stand waiting at the finish line, each with a distinctive cry recognised by their dog, clanging food bowls and bells and whistling in their attempts to bring their hound home first. A winning trail hound is a valuable and much prized animal. Local bookies do brisk trade, with plenty of punters willing to risk a few pounds on a bet.

Puppies are trained from six months old. One person holds the dog while a colleague walks ahead dragging a trail rag or "bait" of meat or cake; then at about 200 paces they call the puppy, which thus learns to associate the scent on the ground with the bait.

PLATE 42

CRUMMOCK WATER AND BUTTERMERE

These two lakes in the north-west were probably linked in an earlier age.
They sit amongst high mountains and are quiet and secluded.

The name Crummock, given the shape of this lake, probably comes from the Gaelic word "cromach", meaning a crook. In windy weather, both Buttermere and Crummock Water can appear rough and wild but, in great contrast, they are calm and beautiful in fine weather. In 1905 there was a boat-landing on Crummock Water so that ladies and gentlemen could be rowed across the lake from the hamlet of Buttermere to see Scale Force, and bathers regularly braved its cold waters.

Scale Force is the highest waterfall in the Lake District, with a single drop of 170 feet. It is hidden away in a deep tree-lined gorge on the way from Crummock Water to Red Pike on land now owned by the National Trust. Wordsworth described it as "a fine chasm, with a lofty, though but slender, fall of water".

Overlooking Buttermere is Haystacks, a favourite fell of Alfred Wainwright, who died in 1991 and whose ashes are scattered there. Black Beck runs down its side in a dizzyingly steep channel. Above lie Blackbeck Tarn and the intriguing Innominate Tarn, for so long unnamed that its lack of name has now identified it in perpetuity. To complete the tally of interesting placenames, Sour Milk Gill pours torrents of foamy water into the foot of Buttermere.

PLATE 43

HEAD OF BUTTERMERE

Buttermere and its neighbours Crummock Water and Loweswater were carved out
thousands of years ago by the same glacier.

Buttermere was a very fashionable tourist destination at the end of the 19th century, being a beautiful and secluded lake surrounded by dramatic fells. Well-dressed visitors would regularly visit it in their carriages, as Honister Pass, the road leading to Buttermere from Borrowdale, though long and steep, was perfectly manageable by horse and carriage.

The tiny church in Buttermere was built in 1841. It was too small to merit a clergyman, so a reader was appointed and paid 20 shillings a year. He also received a pair of clogs and a "hodden sark" (thick shirt), and rights of goosegate (grazing geese on the common) and whittlegate (eating his meals with the farms in the parish).

This too is the hamlet where Mary Robinson lived, the renowned "Beauty of Buttermere" who worked as a maidservant at the Fish Inn. In 1802 she married Alexander Augustus Hope, who turned out to be an imposter and bigamist; he was subsequently hanged at Carlisle, though for forgery rather than bigamy. Her story has been told in several novels, most recently by Melvyn Bragg in *The Maid of Buttermere*.

PLATE 44

HONISTER PASS AND BUTTERMERE

Honister Pass, leading from Seatoller to Buttermere, was once used for carrying slate down from the mine at the summit of the pass. In 1893, eight cottages were built in the area for slate workers.

At the summit of Honister Pass was one of the three most important slate mines in Lakeland. In the 18th century, the slate was carried by packhorse through Wasdale to the coast. Later a system of sleds was used to transport the slate down the hillside.

To make transport easier in the 19th century, a railway was proposed which would extend from Braithwaite near Keswick to the top of the pass. This was prevented by local opposition headed by the indefatigable Canon Rawnsley, one of the founders of the National Trust. However, a system of short gravity-driven railways was developed in the 1890s to bring slate down from the mines. Slate workers spent the whole working week up on Honister, housed in rough huts. Until 1914 they were still using carrier pigeons to send messages down the valley to their wives and families.

Alpine ladies mantle, *Alchemilla alpina*, can be found by the roadside at Honister, as can meadowsweet, *Filipendula ulmaria*. Popularly named Queen of the Meadows, meadowsweet has a sweet aroma and was often used as a floor covering. Its flowers were used medicinally for the treatment of rheumatism, and its roots were a source of black dye.

PLATE 45

THE BORROWDALE YEWS (EVENING)

Three very old yew trees stand on a steep hillside with the Maiden Moor ridge beyond.
A few goats graze peacefully under the trees.

These yews are the remains of what Wordsworth admired as being, even in his time, trees of great antiquity. He called them "the fraternal four of Borrowdale". One of the four succumbed to the Great Storm of 1868; the other three still stand, even though the largest and grandest, on its own just south of the other two, lost a major limb in another storm in 2000.

Yews (*Taxus baccata*) can live for well over a thousand years, and it is difficult to date them because their annual growth rings can rarely be counted as with other trees; the Borrowdale yews are thought to be between 500 and 600 years old. Yew wood was traditionally used for longbows, because yew wood is strong and pliant.

The berries of this tree are poisonous to people and animals, as the seeds contain a poisonous alkaloid, though deer can and do browse on the young seedlings, and birds eat the fruit without harm, as the seeds pass straight through them. Birds depositing seeds here perhaps accounts for the existence of the Borrowdale yews.

Poets, including Wordsworth and Tennyson, were fascinated by yew trees. William Watson (1858–1935), a Yorkshire poet, wrote:

> Old emperor Yew, fantastic sire,
> Girt with thy guard of dotard kings,
> What ages hast thou seen retire
> Into the dust of alien things?

PLATE 46

LODORE AND DERWENTWATER
(A SUMMER'S MORN)

This evocative picture shows the southern end of Derwentwater and its high fells
with the great waterfall of Lodore tumbling down the mountainside.

Robert Southey, a resident of Keswick, and one-time Poet Laureate, was once asked by his son to write a poem about how the water comes down at Lodore. Southey obliged with a long poem in which he used upwards of fifty verbs describing what the water does, and laid the poem out in the pattern of a waterfall. Celia Fiennes, (1662–1741), an early traveller, described the falls as where "severall springs … meet with stones and rocks … they come with more violence that gives a pleasing sound and murmuring noise".

A comic postcard of 1900 shows a dry-season tourist sitting on a rock, having failed to discover the waterfall; he asks a local woman "How does the water come down at Lodore?" "Indeed sir", she replies with a toss of her bonnet, "You may well seek Lodore, for you're sitting upon it". This describes well how the Lodore Falls are subject to variations in quantity of water, from "foaming with fury" (Thomas Gray) to almost indistinguishable in dry weather.

At this end of Derwentwater a floating island occasionally appears, then disappears again within a few weeks. This is a submerged mass of floating vegetation which in hot weather produces methane gas, causing it to rise to the surface.

PLATE 47

DERWENTWATER, FROM CASTLE HEAD
(A BRIGHT MORNING)

This view looks towards the southern end of Derwentwater on a sunny morning.
A bird, perhaps a hawk, sits on the edge of the crag in front of slender pine trees.

The distant fells, including Castle Crag, are what could be described as "dreadful" in the sense used by early tourists — literally filling them with dread. The fells appear wild and unwelcoming, closing up the entrance to the valley beyond the lake as if protecting it.

Lodore Falls can be seen in the far distance, falling from a steep rocky face. The narrow and spectacular entrance to upper Borrowdale, seen behind the rightmost pine tree, is known as the Jaws of Borrowdale. The valley has the reputation of being one of the craggiest and rainiest in the Lake District.

Beyond Lodore is the tiny hamlet of Watendlath, reached by a narrow winding road which crosses the picturesque Ashness Bridge and passes the famous "surprise view" of Derwentwater. Watendlath, with its little tarn and surrounding cottages and farm now owned by the National Trust, is still — as it was in 1905 — a popular spot for visitors. It is the setting for the novel *Judith Paris*, part of *The Herries Chronicle* by Hugh Walpole.

Watendlath. Borrowdale.

PLATE 48

BY THE SHORES OF DERWENTWATER

The view is of Skiddaw from the western side of Derwentwater, with Blencathra in the distance
and an island on the lake just visible. Three naked bathers sit by the edge of the lake.

Along the western side of Derwentwater is Brandelhow Woods, a grassy shoreline with a pleasant walk along it. Brandelhow Park was the first National Trust property in the Lake District, purchased in 1904.

One of the islands on this lake is called St Herbert's Isle because St Herbert, a hermit priest, lived there alone until his death during the 7th century. Each year he went to visit St Cuthbert of Northumbria, whom he greatly admired for his saintliness. It is said that St Herbert asked St Cuthbert to pray that the two of them might die on the same day, and it is recorded that he was granted his request, St Cuthbert on Lindisfarne and St Herbert on St Herbert's Isle both dying on 20 March 687. For centuries afterwards there was an annual pilgrimage by boat to the island, led by the Vicar of Crosthwaite, in which monks from Lindisfarne took part.

Another island, once called Vicar's Island but re-named Derwent Isle, was bought by Joseph Pocklington ("Lord Pocky") in 1778. He was an extravagant character who became famous for the "Regattas" that he held on the lake for his friends, consisting of noisy mock battles and huge firework displays. These became established outings for sightseers at the time.

PLATE 49

GRANGE IN BORROWDALE
(EARLY MORNING)

Grange-in-Borrowdale is a hamlet on the River Derwent, south of Derwentwater,
characterised by its two-arch humpbacked bridge. The hill towering above is Goat Crag.

The impressive double-arched bridge was built in 1675, but Garnge's origins are much earlier; in medieval times the monks of Furness Abbey, owners of this part of the valley, built an outlying farm or grange here, giving it its name. At that time Borrowdale people, with their traditional country ways, were often the subject of mockery by Keswick people, being thought of as simple-minded.

A well-known tourist attraction in the area is the Bowder Stone (named after Balder, son of Odin), an enormous rock the size of a house left behind by an ice age glacier. It perches precariously on one edge over a steep slope, and appears to be about to topple over. It has, however, been in this position for thousands of years. As in 1905, visitors can still climb a wooden ladder and stand on top; today however the view is obscured by trees planted in the mid-20th century.

This whole area was once a source of a substance called wad, otherwise known as black lead or graphite. It was first used to mark sheep; later the Keswick pencil-making industry was founded upon it. It was used in foundries for lining mouldings for cannons and became very valuable. Men working with it were regularly searched when leaving the factory, but despite this much smuggling and selling went on in the back streets of Keswick. This is thought to be the origin of the phrase "black market".

PLATE 50

CROSTHWAITE CHURCH, KESWICK

Crosthwaite Church, on the edge of Keswick, has several famous names associated with it,
and is the burial place of the Poet Laureate, Robert Southey.

Canon Hardwicke Drummond Rawnsley, indefatigable guardian of Lake District landscape, was Vicar of St Kentigern's, Crosthwaite from 1883 to 1917. He was one of three people responsible for founding the National Trust in 1895. His wife Edith co-founded the Keswick Society of Industrial Arts; she designed the church main gates and the very striking brasswork on the reredos.

The church dates from 1523, and is unique in England in having a full set of 16th-century consecration crosses. In former times, when consecrating a church, a bishop would anoint the walls in twelve places marked by crosses, representing the number of disciples of Jesus. At Crosthwaite there are nine of these inside the church and three outside, all of which were rediscovered in 1915 after the removal of roughcast plaster.

In 1844 the church underwent restoration, at which time seventy sackfuls of bones were removed from beneath the organ.

Jonathan Otley (1766–1856), a watchmaker who was one of the first people to write about the geology of the Lake District in a scientific way, regularly attended Crosthwaite Church. He was a very shy man, and always sat in a single, inaccessible pew by a pillar.

The 18th-century Poet Laureate, Robert Southey, lived in Keswick. He died in 1843, and was buried at Crosthwaite where there is a marble monument to him.

PLATE 51

DRUID CIRCLE, NEAR KESWICK (MOONLIGHT)

A romantic, not to say slightly sinister, view of Castlerigg Stone Circle
near Keswick, with Blencathra or Saddleback mounting guard behind.

It is a stirring experience to see this dramatic stone circle by moonlight. Thought to be a thousand years older than Stonehenge, it dates from 3000 to 2500 B.C. John Keats wrote of it in *Hyperion*, Book 2:

> … like a dismal cirque
> Of Druid stones, upon a forlorn moor,
> When the chill rain begins at shut of eve,
> In dull November …

The circle consists of 38 stones of various sizes and shapes; they are all rough boulders, some standing over 5 feet in height, although some have fallen. It has been estimated there were originally 41 stones, so Castlerigg is relatively well preserved when compared with other circles in the British Isles. Its purpose is unknown. Many of the stones of Castlerigg seem to reflect features in the surrounding hills, suggesting an interplay between the sacred space and the landscape beyond. Local legends say the stones are men petrified for their sins, or that the stones are uncountable.

Castlerigg was one of first monuments to be protected under the Ancient Monuments Protection Act of 1868. Hundreds of tourists came to see it, some carving their initials on the stones. Canon Rawnsley ensured the survival of the stone circle by directing its purchase for the National Trust in 1913.

Blencathra, the mountain in the background, is colloquially known as Saddleback because it looks from some aspects as if you could throw a leg over it and ride off into the sunset.

PLATE 52

FALCON CRAG, DERWENTWATER

This impressive crag, part of the ridge of the Central Fells
is seen here from the lake shoreline.

Today Falcon Crag is a favourite with climbers, Chock Gully being one of the Lake District's classic winter climbs. In earlier times, however, the crags were considered "horrid" in the literal sense of the word. Typical of the way early visitors saw the Lake District is an engraving of 1767 by Thomas Smith, which depicts Derwentwater in a way that has never been seen except in the imagination of the artist. The engraving emphasises the drama of the scene. Two people stand under a dead tree with tortured branches reaching out to them, the lake is surrounded by craggy mountains, and the sky is a mass of moving storm clouds, though in the foreground cows graze peacefully enough and a man is venturing forth onto the water in a boat.

By the time of Alfred Heaton Cooper's painting, however, the first climbers were pioneering routes up the crags, paving the way for the many walkers and climbers who today keep the local mountain rescue team busy when they fail to return safely to the safety of the valley.

A little way north of this scene, on the lake shore, is Friar's Crag, famous for its wonderful view down the lake, and for the strong impression it made upon the young John Ruskin, whose memorial stone stands amid the trees there.

PLATE 53

THE VALE OF ST JOHN, NEAR KESWICK

The Vale of St John, also called St John's in the Vale, is in the valley of St John's Beck
which rises from Thirlmere and becomes the River Glenderamackin at Threlkeld.

The Church of St John is in this vale; there has been worship here for 400 years though the present church building only dates from 1845.

Tewet Tarn, on top of Low Rigg, from which the views open out across the Vale of St John, has an excellent view of Skiddaw and Blencathra. The nearby village of Threlkeld once thrived as a mining community, but all five mines are now closed. Its name, originating from Old Norse, means Thrall's well.

The Castle Rock of Triermaine is a particularly distinctive rock formation in St John's in the Vale that has the appearance of a ruined castle but is, in fact, nothing but a mass of fallen rocks. Like the "Druid" circles it has gathered legends around it, chiefly that the castle is transformed into a rock pile when humans approach it. Only certain magically endowed people like King Arthur can see the castle, no one else. Scotland's great romantic writer, Sir Walter Scott, wrote a poem about it, one of his Arthurian ballads called "The Bridal of Triermain".

> The narrow dale lay smooth and still, …
> But, midmost of the vale, a mound
> Arose with airy turrets crown'd.
> Buttress and ramparts circling bound,
> And mighty keep and tower.

Castle Rocks, St John's Vale, English Lakes

PLATE 54

DERWENTWATER AND BASSENTHWAITE LAKE, FROM HIGH LODORE

This view of Derwentwater with Bassenthwaite beyond from south to north,
shows most of the lake and the striking range of fells at the northern end.

The island in the lake is St Herbert's Isle. This prospect of the lake is both unexpected and dramatic, beautifully set off by the framework of silver birches.

Early visitors to the Lake District were largely overawed by the experience, and found the fells in particular intimidating. In 1778 Thomas West, a Jesuit priest living in Furness, wrote a *Guide to the Lakes* that described the experiences of new travellers to the area. His guide abounds with words like "terror", "dark cliffs", "jaws" and "dreadful". He quotes a Dr Brown of Wigton who describes the surroundings of Derwentwater as "beauty, horror and immensity".

People were excited by these early guide books; they came in search of drama and awe-inspiring nature and as soon as the railways arrived in the mid-1800s mass tourism began.

One of Thomas West's ideas was that of the "station". This is West's word for a viewpoint, or a place where the visitor might get the "best" view. One of these stations still stands, a tower, now almost a ruin, among the trees on a hillside at Claife above the Ferry House on Windermere. The way early guidebook writers recommended visitors should see the Lakes was very prescriptive: they had to follow the stations and use a "Claude glass", a slightly tinted convex mirror which shaped a large scene into a neat view.

PLATE 55

BASSENTHWAITE LAKE (A BREEZY MORN)

This lake is the answer to the question "How many lakes are there in the Lake District?"
Answer "One, Bassenthwaite". All the rest are waters or meres.

Bassenthwaite as shown in Alfred Heaton Cooper's painting looks cold and choppy, but today it is one of the more peaceful lakes despite the sailing, windsurfing and fishing that take place and the A66 which runs along the western shore of the lake. Woods fringe parts of its shores on both sides, and recently ospreys nested at Bassenthwaite and bred young for the first time in England for 150 years. The pattern has now been repeated for several years, with the adults and their young migrating to Africa at the end of the summer and returning to Bassenthwaite each spring. A webcam captures images from the nest, and visitors to a viewing centre at nearby Dodd Wood can watch the ospreys without disturbing them.

St Bega's Church stands on the shore of Bassenthwaite not far from Mirehouse. It is dedicated to the daughter of a 12th-century Irish chieftain who ran away from Ireland to Cumbria to avoid an arranged marriage, and settled here to renounce the world and serve God. A bracelet of hers bearing an image of the Cross was used for miraculous healing.

John Betjeman said of this area "A perfect English harmony of man and nature … All around sketches a lost landscape of pasture and river. O fortunatus nimium!" – of which a very modern rendering might be "Oh, it's all too much!"

PLATE 56

BASSENTHWAITE LAKE AND SKIDDAW

A view of the familiar shape of Skiddaw from across Bassenthwaite, with
St Bega's Church, otherwise known as St Bees, just visible.

It is still customary to celebrate great national events with a chain of fires on beacons or significant hill tops – Skiddaw is one of these beacon hills. In 1833 the Victorian historian Lord Macaulay, referred to the 200th anniversary in 1788 of the defeat of the Spanish Armada in 1588, wrote:

> Till Skiddaw saw the fire that burned on Gaunt's embattled
>   pile [Lancaster Castle],
> And the red glare on Skiddaw roused the burghers of Carlisle.

On the back shoulder of Skiddaw is a solitary building, Skiddaw House, which now belongs to the Youth Hostels Association. During Victorian times it was known as the most isolated building in all England, standing as it does high up on a vast fellside with no other building in view. Walpole set his novel *The Fortress* there.

Mirehouse stands on the eastern shore of Bassenthwaite, a 17th-century house and home of James Spedding, who numbered among his close friends Alfred Lord Tennyson and Edward Fitzgerald, translator of the *Rubaiyat of Omar Khayyam*. After losing his close friend Arthur Hallam in 1833, Tennyson spent some time at Mirehouse; it is thought that he was inspired here to set his *Morte d'Arthur*, with its obvious reference to his friend, on Bassenthwaite Lake. The Speddings still live at Mirehouse, and open it to the public at certain times.

PLATE 57

RAVEN CRAG, THIRLMERE

Thirlmere supplies water to South Lancashire, and has a dead, depressing air, though the little
western road by Armboth is very beautiful, with magnificent rock formations.

When Manchester decided to draw water from Thirlmere in 1876 the *Gentleman's Magazine* wrote: "May Cottonopolis be sent nearer home for its water supply." The Thirlmere Defence Association was formed and many literary personalities of the day spoke against the project, Ruskin, Carlyle, Matthew Arnold and William Morris among them. Canon Rawnsley famously changed sides and finished by officiating at the opening ceremony in 1892 with a prayer.

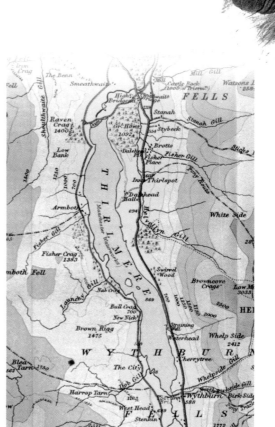

An agreement to plant native trees was apparently ignored, and the area became dead, dark and depressing with solid ranks of fir trees hiding the shapes of the hills, until Susan Johnson, daughter of H.H. Symonds, Founder of the Friends of the Lake District, sued and won her case in the 1990s. Now only native trees are planted and the area has become more interesting within the limits of its function. There is sometimes an ugly waterline owing to the rise and fall in the level of the water.

The Launchy Gill Nature Reserve has been created on the western side of the lake; it contains indigenous oak and birch woodlands and some rare plants in the gills, for which reason gill scrambling, which has become very popular in parts of Lakeland, is discouraged. Raven Crag, named after the birds that once nested on it, is impressive, rearing up over the western lakeside road.

PLATE 58

THIRLMERE AND HELVELLYN

Helvellyn, one of the most popular hills in the Lake District for walkers, extends for most of the length of Thirlmere's eastern side and is seen at its best viewed from the opposite shore of Thirlmere.

Many people who walk seriously in the Lake District are tempted to try Striding Edge, that challenging "tight-rope" walk to the top of Helvellyn along a ridge with plunging slopes on either side. The story of Charles Gough, who fell to his death in 1803 (before there was any suitable equipment for such a hazardous activity), is famous for the fact that his faithful dog was found three months later keeping guard over his bones. Cynics may scoff but, from the age of Romanticism, Walter Scott's words on the matter are touching:

How long didst thou think that his silence was slumber?
When the wind waved his garment how oft didst thou start?
How many long days and long weeks didst thou number,
Ere he faded before thee, the friend of thy heart?

A stone memorial was placed there to Gough in 1890.

For many years there has been a tradition of climbing Helvellyn by night – by an easy route – to greet Midsummer Day. Some people sleep on the summit overnight to see the sun rise the next morning.

Thirlmere, once called Leathes Water, stretches along the western flank of Helvellyn. A legend exists about the Black Dog of Thirlmere, which, if seen swimming in the lake, is a portent of evil.

PLATE 59

HAWESWATER

This view of Haweswater is no longer to be seen. Formerly two small lakes,
High Water and Low Water, the lake has been a reservoir since 1941.

Haweswater was turned into a reservoir by building a 120ft high dam, flooding the valley, and drowning the small hamlet of Mardale which consisted of nine inhabited houses, four farms, a church, a school, and the Dun Bull public house. The population was around forty when the plan was mooted in 1929. As work on the reservoir progressed, bodies from the churchyard were taken away for reburial. During the drought year of 1976 part of the village, including the church, again became visible, and visitors came to see the ruins of the drowned village. As we experience more drought years, this will no doubt become a regular occurrence.

The Dun Bull was greatly missed by local shepherds, having been a major place for shepherds' meets, periodic gatherings to collect stray sheep and enjoy a social

get-together. A famous meet was held until 1835 on top of High Street, south-west of the reservoir, and later at the Kirkstone Pass Inn and at the Dun Bull.

Norman Nicholson (1914–87), the local poet who lived all his life in Millom on the west Cumbrian coast, said of the reservoir "what we see is not a dale with a lake in it, but a group of fells plunged up to the waist in cold water".

In the Middle Ages, Latin was taught at Measand House, west of the lake, and it is recorded that ploughmen spoke to their horses in Latin. A grammar school was founded there in 1711, to teach the classics.

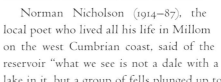

CROWN & MITRE HOTEL,
Haweswater, PENRITH.

The only Hotel in the fine Mountain District, lying between Shap, Haweswater, Mardale, and Ullswater.
Bracing Air. Charming Scenery.
Good Fishing in River and Lake.
Parties met at Penrith and Shap stations when required.
Telegraphic Address: "Hotel, Bampton, Westmoreland." M. J. CLARK, Proprietress.

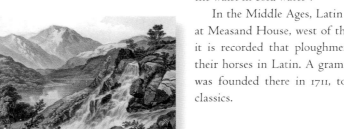

PLATE 60

SHAP ABBEY

This is all that remains of Shap Abbey, of the Premonstratensian (White Canons) order founded in 1199. The Abbey was closed under the Dissolution of 1540.

Most of the rest of the abbey buildings, though reduced to low walls, can be seen today, and the tower still stands as shown in Alfred's painting. The outlines of the cloisters and dormitories also remain.

The ruins stand in a pretty valley by the River Lowther. About a mile from the abbey is the hamlet of Keld with half a dozen houses and the tiny Keld Chapel, open to the public by application at a local house. This was built in the 15th century by the monks as a place of worship for the farmers in that area, and now belongs to the National Trust.

After the Dissolution, stone from the abbey buildings was taken to build Lowther Castle in Westmorland, the first of two castles built by the Earls of Lonsdale in 1682. The second, an elaborate "neo-Gothick" building, was started in 1806, to replace one which had been destroyed by fire. It was in 1897 that a Shap mason removed the last stone from the grange at the abbey.

The Shap granite works are still active today. The Albert Memorial, London Bridge, Holborn Viaduct and the bollards in front of St Paul's Cathedral all contain Shap granite. There were also important wells at Shap, producing medicinal waters for "ascorbitic disorders".

PLATE 61

ULLSWATER, FROM GOWBARROW PARK (A SULTRY JUNE MORN)

One of the most beautiful of the English Lakes, surrounded by gentle fells and a pleasing shoreline.

In the foreground are wild hyacinths and primroses, and the deer are enjoying the warm June day. Red deer are common in the Lake District and roam freely. Deer forests were important in the Cumbrian landscape of early times; they were protected by forest law and maintained by their owners for hunting. Many deer parks that still exist today were originally deer forests for hunting.

Wordsworth's most famous poem, "The Daffodils", was written in his early years in the Lake District, and it is generally believed that it was inspired by a description of this Ullswater scene written by his sister, Dorothy. In his later life some of Wordsworth's poetry was less inspired. It once evoked the following comment from a certain John Squire, wishing to convey that Wordsworth did not always get it right:

Two voices are there, one is of the deep,
And one is of an old half-witted sheep.
And Wordsworth, both are thine.

To the west of Gowbarrow Park is Aira Force, a dramatic waterfall; close by is a Gothic folly built as a hunting lodge by the Duke of Norfolk. Known as Lyulph's Tower, it has been described by the poet Norman Nicholson as "a fortified china cabinet".

PLATE 62

ULLSWATER, SILVER BAY

A calm scene with the silvery lake and distant purple hills
reflected darkly in the still water. A boat drifts lazily.

The name Ullswater is almost certainly derived from the Old Norse word "ulf" or wolf, an element which crops up in many Lakeland placenames. Other suggested derivations include "Lyulph's Water", Lyulph being the name of the first Baron Greystoke of ancient history, and "Ulfor's Water", a name of older Norse origin.

Several famous 18th-century painters favoured Ullswater with their skills, among them William Green (1760–1823) and Joseph Wright of Derby (1734–97). Green's painting, shown to the right, depicts a grand but stylised landscape which contrasts with the altogether gentler, more naturalistic scenes painted by Alfred Heaton Cooper, which were done "en plein air" from nature itself. Both however convey the grandeur of the scene and, in the case of Green's depiction, a little of the "horror" he must have felt.

The development and growing popularity of landscape painting in the 19th century, combined with the fact that the materials became easier to use, completely changed the way artists painted. Detailed sketches were made out of doors and the final work completed in the studio. Unlike the work of more dramatic painters such as Green in earlier times, reliance was placed more on the sketches than on the imagination. Alfred Heaton Cooper's work reflects these fundamental changes in English landscape painting.

PLATE 63

ULLSWATER:
THE SILVER STRAND (AFTERGLOW)

A beautiful curving shoreline on a smooth lake with a distant sailing boat
and remote islet. The setting sun is tinting the distant hill.

Rhododendrons are shown in the foreground of this painting, shrubs which were brought back by 19th-century plant hunters from Nepal and Tibet. They were introduced into Lakeland gardens, where they have since taken over vast areas of land.

This view is from a curve in the lake looking north, beyond which the lake swings over to the east. Ullswater is a very long lake with three marked bends and an interesting shoreline. Steamers ply from end to end of the lake giving tourists a view of the changing scene. Helvellyn's Striding Edge can clearly be seen from certain points.

Patterdale, at the southern end of the lake, is a shortened version of St Patrick's Dale, with St Patrick's Church and a holy well. Patterdale Hall, originally a 17th-century building, once belonged to the Mounsey family, who were known as the "kings" of Patterdale. In the 19th century it became the property of the Marshall family from Leeds, who were friends of the Wordsworths.

The lake contains a rare fish known as the schelly (*Coreganus laveratus*), sometimes called the freshwater herring.

PLATE 64

HAZY TWILIGHT, HEAD OF ULLSWATER

A calm, misty, evening scene in summer with a smooth lake,
rhododendrons, and a lone fisherman enjoying the solitude.

The large hill on the left, Place Fell, has very fine views from its summit. Dorothy and William Wordsworth climbed this fell in 1805 and were shown a ruin, described to them as an ancient chapel, where people used to worship. Dorothy had her doubts and thought it was a mere sheepfold. It is still there, a heap of stones in the shape of a rectangle.

Ullswater is one of the most beautiful of the lakes because of its wide panorama of peaks, its curving shoreline and bays. In the 18th century people discovered that fine echoes could be achieved from the surrounding hills, and would take to the lake in boats to produce loud noises to awaken them: discharges of cannon were popular, while others suggested that musical instruments might produce a better result.

The rare arctic char used to be found in this lake but, even as early as 1905, they had been destroyed by pollution from the mines at Greenside. During the Wordsworths' visit in 1805 they saw a fishing boat with a net containing hundreds of fish "leaping in their prison". They called them "skellies".

PLATE 65

A MOUNTAIN PATH, SANDWICK, ULLSWATER

Sandwick is a small bay with a farm on the eastern shore of Ullswater,
most often reached today by the lakeshore footpath from How Town to Patterdale.

The path follows the edge of the lake at both high and low levels, through fields or on steep banks such as here, with beautiful views in fine weather of the changing vista of the hills. Notice the outcrops of craggy rock and the small, stunted trees that take root within them. Sheep wander among the rocks.

Elegant steamers, like the one pictured here, have plied the lake for over a century, though they are now no longer powered by steam. A favourite day out starts from Glenridding Pier, cruising down to How Town on the opposite shore and walking the lakeshore path back. In recent years, fellwalking passengers on the Ullswater steamers to How Town have donated hundreds of pounds to mend the lakeshore footpath that their boots have helped to wear out.

Yellow gorse can be seen everywhere. Gorse (*Ulex europaeus*) is a member of the clover and pea, Leguminosae or Fabaceae. A common name for it is "whin" or "furze". The flowers scent the air with a vanilla or coconut fragrance, and there is a saying that "when gorse is out of bloom, kissing's out of season", a reference to the fact that it is one of the few wild flowers to blossom all the year round.

PLATE 66

BROUGHAM CASTLE, PENRITH

Brougham Castle, just south-east of Penrith, was one of the estates of Lady Anne Clifford (1590–1676),
who was celebrated as a wise and benevolent lady of property.

Lady Anne was deeply attached to Brougham where her father was born and her mother died, so when Anne inherited the castle in 1643 she won her heart's desire. The castle was greatly damaged during the Civil War and, from 1651 to 1653, Anne restored it and then moved in. In 1660 the hearth tax records show that Brougham had 30 hearths – rooms with heating, fireplaces or furnaces.

The panorama from the upper storeys at Brougham would have encompassed the rivers Eamont, on the banks of which the castle stands, Lowther and Eden, as well as the Pennine fells and the Lake District mountains.

Lady Anne was nothing if not a hands-on landlord. She celebrated the restoration of Charles II and his birthday on 29 May every year from 1660 and paid for "ye bone fire" by the waterside at Brougham. She was generous to her tenants with money and food, and put on Christmas feasts for them. She died at Brougham in 1676 at the great age of 86. In 1691 the castle was partly demolished and from 1714 any material that could be used from it was sold off. The ruins are now open to visitors during the summer months.

PLATE 67

ANGLE TARN, ESK HAUSE

This striking picture shows Angle Tarn lying under the crags of Bow Fell,
the scene softened by the sheep grazing on the grassy bank below.

Esk Hause (the word "hause" meaning a neck of land between mountain ridges) is a crossroads on the path linking Great Langdale with Wasdale. Wainwright disputes with the Ordnance Survey the actual location of Esk Hause, but no doubt the average walker is happy with it as long as it leads them where they want to go, though it is easy to go astray here and descend into Borrowdale instead of Langdale and vice versa.

Angle Tarn, a wild remnant of the ice age, looks rather dark and sinister here, but in summer is a welcoming place. It is a favourite place to swim naked after a strenuous walk, being so isolated and unvisited.

Bow Fell towers above Angle Tarn, a peaked hill with interesting rock formations on top. Because the access is straightforward, it is a very popular hill for walkers starting from Great Langdale who climb up out of the valley by way of a gentle slope called The Band. The views of the Langdale Pikes from here are wonderful. The summit of Bow Fell is rocky and wild enough to be enjoyed as a satisfying challenge by those who prefer to scramble rather than rock climb.

PLATE 68

DALEGARTH FORCE, ESKDALE

Dalegarth Falls, also known as Dalegarth Force, stand above Dalegarth Hall,
an early fortified manor house with a pele tower.

Dalegarth is in Eskdale and is the terminus of the miniature railway, Laal Ratty, which runs from Ravenglass on the coast to the village of Boot. "Laal" is Cumbrian dialect for "little". This railway, built in 1875, which was originally constructed to carry iron ore and granite, soon became a trippers' jaunt — the Victorians loved it and railway enthusiasts today take it very seriously. Everything on the fifteen-inch gauge is exactly to scale.

Eskdale

Dalegarth Falls are a very pretty example of a Cumbrian waterfall, 40 feet high, locked within a rocky channel, foaming white in a steep, straight drop. Dalegarth Hall, the former fortified manor house, was the home of the Stanley family, and an alternative name for the Dalegarth Falls is Stanley Gill Force. Fortified manor houses are found everywhere in the English Lake District, even as far down as south Westmorland, not just in the borders where it might be thought they were needed to defend against Scottish incursion.

One of the loveliest waterfall walks in the Lake District is through Stanley Gill Force Woods, where a network of paths and bridges enable visitors to see the falls to best advantage. The woods have recently been cleared of rhododendrons.

PLATE 69

BLEA TARN AND LANGDALE PIKES

This is a classic view of Blea Tarn and across Great Langdale to the familiar shapes,
always recognisable, of the Langdale Pikes.

Wordsworth called Blea Tarn "a liquid pool that glittered in the sun". A road from Little Langdale to Great Langdale passes this tarn, which is set high among a group of smaller hills, and from its shores can be seen those giants the Langdale Pikes, on the opposite side of the Langdale Valley.

Polished stone axes are known to have been made by the neolithic inhabitants of Langdale, and an axe factory was discovered in 1947 on the screes descending from Pike of Stickle to the valley. These skilful people created the axes in situ from a kind of volcanic rock found on the fell and then sent them to the coast. Here the axeheads were polished and finished with sand from the seashore before being exported to Ireland and even to Europe.

Around the tarn are rhododendron bushes with their deep purple flowers, and heather, which as well as looking pretty was used for fuel, roof-thatching, and to provide aromatic animal bedding. It was also employed in ale-brewing.

PLATE 70

A SUDDEN SHOWER, BLEA TARN

Blea Tarn, or Blue Tarn, so called because of the colour of the water,
is a name given to several "small waters" situated high in the Lakeland hills.

In this picture the walker will recognise the atmosphere of a sudden heavy shower on a sunny day, and the vestiges of a rainbow. The raindrops are almost individually visible. It is said that the sun sets between the two Pikes shown here on Midsummer Day.

The grazing sheep are probably Herdwicks, the breed best adapted to some of the rougher parts of Lakeland, being hardy and nimble enough to climb rough crags. Their wool, being dark grey or black, cannot be dyed and so is less suitable for clothing. It can be used for hard-wearing rugs or carpets. Herdwick lamb and mutton is widely eaten in the Lake District and is now marketed further afield. Mutton is the basis of hotpot, a popular local stew of meat and potatoes baked slowly in the oven. Karel Čapek (1890–1938), the Czech writer, said of these sheep: "They graze on silken lawns … Nobody watches them and they spend their time in feeding, sleeping and divine pondering." Apart from the silken lawns (where did he see these in Lakeland?) this probably applies still to most sheep, fortunately for them. Up in these hills is also the place to hear curlew with their bewitching, cascading notes, plovers, and lapwings or peewits, which some people locally call "tewits".

THE ENGLISH LAKES, WINDERMERE.

A. HEATON COOPER -

PLATE 71

KIRKSTONE PASS AND BROTHERS' WATER

This view shows to good advantage the kind of rugged country to be expected over the famed Kirkstone Pass.
The road is long, steep and sinuous from the top of the pass right down to Brotherswater.

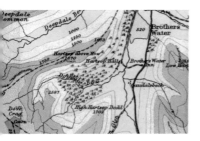

The Kirk Stone, the large steeple-shaped boulder the pass is reputedly named after, is seen to best advantage when climbing the road going south and nearing the summit. The Kirkstone Pass Inn stands on the summit, and is where shepherds' meets were held until 1835. A note in the visitors' book for 11 November 1905 reads:

> The Kirkstone Inn is hard to come at,
> But me and Maud have reached its summit.

Kaiser Wilhelm crossed the pass with his entourage in 1895 – Beatrix Potter was an observer at this event.

The name of the lake, Brotherswater, is in some dispute. Dorothy Wordsworth tells of two brothers who, three centuries ago, were skating on it, fell through the ice and were drowned. Others say the lake's name was originally Broadwater or Broaderwater. It is unusually square in shape.

Two roads run to the top of the pass from the south. One is through Troutbeck and is longer, though easier. The second, short and straight up, almost literally, from Ambleside and called "the Struggle", is banned to heavy traffic. On 8 June 2002 a coach defied the ban and its brakes failed while descending "the Struggle". The vehicle crashed on to its side after colliding with a garden wall and four elderly passengers were seriously injured.

PLATE 72

STEPPING-STONES, FAR EASEDALE, GRASMERE

Far Easedale Gill runs down to Grasmere from its source on top of Grasmere Common.

Easedale runs from Grasmere, by way of Goody Bridge, up by the side of Sour Milk Gill, so called because it is always white and foaming as it drops steeply downhill, and up to Easedale Tarn. The latter is a calm place surrounded by green fells, on the route to the Langdale Pikes and Dungeon Ghyll.

Nineteenth-century tourists used to take guides up onto to the fells; one famous Easedale guide was William "Swanney" Wilson, born in 1843, who started guiding visitors at the age of fifteen. He continued doing this until he was an old man, also giving lessons in rock climbing. People would meet him by arrangement at Easedale Tarn by his little bothy, where he would entertain them with tales of the mountains and give them refreshments, then take them by pony across the fells. His bothy was called the Tourists' Rest.

The famous "Guides Races", which still take place at Lakeland Sports events, originated as races up the fells held amongst the guides. Nowadays, fell runners from a wide area flock to the Lakes to compete in these exacting and strenuous races.

PLATE 73

LITTLE LANGDALE TARN

High fells shield Little Langdale Tarn, while the stream that eventually becomes the River Brathay finds its way from the tarn by way of two impressive waterfalls, Colwith and Skelwith.

A famous packhorse bridge leads into Little Langdale – Slater's Bridge used to convey slate when the industry was in full swing. It is four feet wide with no parapet walling, to allow for wide loads. On the track approaching the tarn it is possible to enter a vast, towering slate cave, called The Cathedral, blasted out of the rock. A huge "window" in one wall, open to the skies, sheds much-needed light for those exploring the cave.

The area of Little and Great Langdale was the haunt of a famous fiddler, William or Bill Irwin, who was leader of the "Lakeland Fiddlers" during the 19th century. Born in 1822, he died of typhoid in 1889 and is buried in Chapel Stile graveyard. He played the fiddle at village inns and dances, and was also a well-known folk music composer.

A local custom called "hunsopping" was popular at Christmas, when the group went calling at houses and playing a tune called "Hunsop through the Wood" to each member of the household. This bizarre word apparently grew out of the phrase "the hunt is up", a call to get people to join the hunt at "break of day" as John Peel did.

PLATE 74

ELTERWATER AND LANGDALE PIKES

Elterwater, lake of the swans, seems an appropriate setting for these gentle creatures.
A favourite view of the Langdale Pikes, one peak rearing up over the other like a lion's head, is seen from this lake.

Silverthwaite, an interesting property now owned by the National Trust , was built in this valley in 1905. The five-bedroomed house was once inhabited by Amy Sharp, a suffragist (not a suffragette, the difference being that whereas suffragettes were prepared to use violence, suffragists simply advocated the extension of the suffrage). She was one of the first women to study at Cambridge, where she was awarded an Upper Second in the Moral Sciences Tripos in 1882. Cambridge, however, did not grant degrees to women, so she had to pay for her degree from Trinity College, Dublin, which she did in 1905.

The house is on the side of a hill in the Langdale Valley and is interesting because of its link with the Arts and Crafts movement, the fireplaces and decorations bearing witness to this.

The clock of Holy Trinity Church in the village of Chapel Stile, Great Langdale, installed in 1858 at a time when this kind of turret clock design was becoming popular, has been called the country cousin of Big Ben. Lord Grimthorpe (1816–1905) was responsible for introducing the turret clock into Britain.

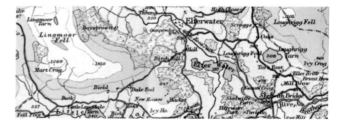

PLATE 75

SEATHWAITE TARN, DUDDON VALLEY

A view of this tarn set deeply under Grey Friar with a heap of rocks resembling
a huge campfire in the foreground, and scattered sheep grazing.

Tarns or "minor waters" in the hills are found aplenty in this area and, unlike the lakes, are hard to distinguish from each other. Often, as here, the tarn is surrounded on three sides by overhanging crags with a fourth side allowing a gentle approach, allowing sheep to graze and drink. The word "tarn" or "tjorn" in Old Norse meant "teardrop" or small lake.

Seathwaite Tarn, now a reservoir for Barrow-in-Furness, lies in the Seathwaite Fells. The lord of the manor had the exclusive rights for fishing in this tarn – among the fish caught here were char, trout and perch.

The hills around the tarn are all called crags, brows, or hows, and they have been given graphic names. Shudderstone How implies shattering rock, while Goat Crag is associated with agility. Tarn Brow conveys hills that are "beetling" or overhanging like those in the picture, and Raven Nest How conjures up the bird that haunts the Tower of London or Edgar Allan Poe's creepy poem.

Bronze age relics have been found around the area near the Duddon, and more than sixty bronze age sites have been excavated in the area between the Duddon and the River Ehen.

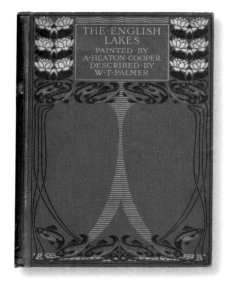

ABOUT THE ORIGINAL BOOK

The English Lakes was an enduring success for A&C Black and Alfred Heaton Cooper, one of the publisher's most faithful artists. It was an early title in the company's growing *20 Shilling Series* which, eventually numbering 92 titles, was to become one of the period's great publishing success stories.

First published in August 1905, in an edition of 3,000 copies plus a large paper signed edition of 250, it was reprinted the same year and in 1908, 1913 (twice) and 1918. A&C Black went on to use the same illustrations in a variety of later books, but also commissioned Heaton Cooper to provide watercolours for books on Ireland, the Isle of Wight, the Isle of Man, Dorset, Somerset, Norfolk and Suffolk, Norway and other places over the next 25 years – a total of more than 400 paintings in more than 30 books.

When *The English Lakes* was commissioned in 1904, Heaton Cooper was struggling to make a living as an artist. A&C Black offered him £200 for the right to reproduce 75 paintings – the originals were always returned to the artist for him/her to sell, although in this instance the publisher wanted to retain one picture. Why they wished to do so is not stated: perhaps for the boardroom wall. The cover design was by A.A. Turbayne, as was usual for most of this series, and was based on ideas from Heaton Cooper.

In a brief memoir written by his son William, also a Lake District painter, William records that "one day in 1904 a director of Blacks the publishers knocked at the cottage door and asked my father to

The first local review of *The English Lakes* in the *Westmorland Gazette* of Saturday 12 August, 1905.

provide 75 illustrations to a book, *The English Lakes*, written by W.T. Palmer. For this he would be paid an outright £150. This was their first ray of real hope. He completed all the paintings within a year and his work began to sell, including one to Harvard University."

The facts are slightly at variance with the publisher's records and nothing in his correspondence suggests that Adam Black ever went to visit his authors or artists, although a firm's representative may have done so. But the visit certainly changed AHC's life for the better. Jane Renouf's biography of the artist refers to 75 illustrations at £3 each, which is probably the correct figure. This included surrender of copyright and allowed subsequent publication of the pictures in various books without further payments. But this was the same deal as was offered to all the firm's artists.

The text of *The English Lakes*, by W.T. Palmer, a journalist on the staff of the *Liverpool Courier*, is notable chiefly for its use of onomatopoeic words that are unlikely to be found elsewhere: sloom, glish, benks, cluthering, dowly, etc.

The A&C Black book about the English Lakes, though by far the most successful, was not the only colour picture book of the period to feature specially commissioned paintings. Its main rival was the smaller and cheaper Blackie title *The English Lakes* written by A.G. Bradley with paintings by E.W. Haslehust, published in 1910. With its last reprinting in 1918, however, the Heaton Cooper book eventually reached a total print run of over 22,000 copies.

A New World of Colour Printing

The late Victorians and Edwardians loved colour, and great strides in printing and ink technology allowed them to have it, breaking free of the limitations of the monotone pages of their parents' generation with their woodcuts and steel engravings. Many of these developments came from Germany, where by the turn of the 19th century there was a lucrative industry in colour postcards, greetings cards, and books containing dozens of colour illustrations.

The challenge and promise of colour were quickly taken up in Britain, where presses — especially in London and Edinburgh — started using the latest technology to print colour plates for a range of reference books.

Until the early 1890s, anyone wanting to print a colour image had to design the images in such a way that the different colours, each printed from its own plate, could easily be separated from each other. Many ways were developed to create subtlety in the use of colour, including engraving fine detail into each colour plate, using separate plates for different tones of the same colour, and hand-finishing each plate after it had been printed. Even so, most colour printing in 1900 was fairly crude, and it is clear — especially under the magnifying glass — that the drive for realistic colour still had some way to go.

The best colour printing in 1900, however, was stunning. In the period between 1900 and 1914, before war dried up ink and machinery supplies from Germany to the rest of the world, printing in colour reached a peak not to be reached again until the 1960s.

How did they achieve this quality? It is important to remember that outdoor colour photography as we know it, using colour film to photograph places and people, was not invented until the 1930s. However, from about 1890 onwards, several processes for making colour photographs of inanimate objects in a studio setting were well advanced, and Edwardian photographers were amazingly inventive.

One of the greatest pioneers was a German emigré, Carl Hentschel, who in the 1890s patented the Hentschel Colourtype Process and set up his company in London's Fleet Street. Hentschel developed a massive camera which used three colour filters — red, green and blue — to capture simultaneous images of any flat colour original. At the same time, developments such as the halftone screen, allowing colour gradation to be printed as an almost imperceptible regular pattern of different-sized dots onto paper, was enabling photographed images to be transferred to paper, both in black and white and in the new three-colour "process" method.

It was now possible to photograph flat objects like paintings, or small groups of objects in a studio setting, in colour. And it was possible to use those images, separated into their three component process colours, to print colour images. It was impossible, however, to make colour photographs of the wide outside world, of cities, mountains and crowds of people. Yet once they had a taste of colour postcards and colour pictures in books, those who could afford to buy such relatively expensive luxuries wanted as much colour as they could get.

The images in the present book demonstrate the many ways in which Edwardian inventors, photographers and publishers strove to give their customers what they so craved — the real world on the printed page in full colour.

The preface to the 1900 seventh edition of *Alpine Flora* written by L. Schröter and Professor Doctor C. Schröter boasts that "special attention has been given to the execution of the illustrations".

A midday feast for a hard-working engraver of the 1900s from *The Penrose's Pictorial Annual* of 1907–8.

Carl Hentschel (top) and the original Three Men in a Boat, Carl Hentschel, George Wingrave, and Jerome himself.

The Chromographoscope (below) invented by du Hauron in 1874 was a dual purpose machine. It could be used as a camera or as an additive viewer.

THE HENTSCHEL THREE-COLOUR PROCESS

Carl Hentschel moved to London from the Russian-Polish city of Lodz with his family in 1868 when he was four years old. Like his father he became an engraver, and by 1900 was an important figure both in colour printing and in London's social life. As well as being an active advocate of his innovative printing process he was a founder member of several clubs including the Playgoer's Club, and as a great friend of Jerome K. Jerome was the model for Harris in Jerome's *Three Men in a Boat.*

Although not the inventor of the three-colour halftone process – it had been developed by Frenchmen Louis du Hauron and Charles Cros and American Frederick Ives in the 1870s – Hentschel's company led the way in using the method on a commercial scale.

The process is well described in Burch's 1906 book *Colour Printing and Colour Printers*: "Once the principle is accepted that any combination of colours can be resolved into its primary elements, it remains only for the photographer to obtain three negatives which automatically dissect the original, making three distinct photographic records of the reds, yellows and blues which enter into the composition. The result is obtained by the use of transparent screens of coloured pigment or liquid, "light filters" as they are technically termed, placed in front of the lens. These filters admit any two of the primary colours and absorb the other one. Three separate screens are employed, each with the lines ruled at a different angle, and when the negative records of the colour analysis are obtained, the three photographs are converted into printing surfaces."

Among Hentschel's growing list of customers was Adam Black, the original "A" of A&C Black, who early on recognised the Colourtype process as the one that would give his publishing company

a head start in the production of colour books. In its time it must have seemed magical that colour plates could be produced to such a high standard and, at only four hours from photograph to finished printing plate, so quickly.

COLOUR POSTCARDS

The first decade of the 20th century was the high tide of the postcard craze, which used the new technologies of colour printing and the halfpenny postcard postage rate to fill Edwardian living rooms with pictures from all over the world. In 1899 the British Post Office gave in to popular pressure to allow postcards to have more than just the address written on the back, which allowed publishers to use all of the picture side to display their design.

By 1904 Raphael Tuck had more than 10,000 different postcard designs, and had launched their Oilette brand based on often very beautiful and original paintings; there would eventually be more than 3,000 different sets of Tuck Oilette postcards. Tuck's range included many postcards taken from illustrations in the A&C Black books; and A&C Black themselves published a similar quantity under their own name.

Postcard publishers rapidly increased production to fill the demand for postcards, these cards being the one product line that constantly pushed colour printing to the limits of what was achievable. Many colour postcards, even of out-of-the-way British scenes, were printed in Germany, or by British companies with German origins. None was more inventive, productive and formative than the London-based company of Raphael Tuck and Sons. Raphael Tuch (his original name) moved to London with his wife and eleven children from Breslau in Prussia in 1865. He opened a small shop in Whitechapel, moving in 1870 to City Road, where he and his sons Adolph, Herman and Gustave helped to develop a range of photographs and Victorian scraps, much of it imported from Germany. In 1871 came the first Christmas card, and in 1876 the coloured oleograph. The breakthrough year for the postcard was 1894, when Tucks produced a card with a vignette of Snowdon in North Wales.

In the first decades of the postcard's life there were three ways of producing a colour image. You either started with a real black and white photograph, and added subtle layers of colour to indicate water or a sunset, or you used traditional colour engravers to create separated colour designs from scratch, or you used the new three-colour process to photograph painted originals. It was this third option that allowed companies like Raphael Tuck and Sons to expand so rapidly, and they were quick to commission a number of excellent artists to create series of paintings specifically for reproduction as postcards.

PHOTOCHROMES

Of all the methods for colourising photographic images before outdoor colour photography, the photochrome process was probably the most successful. The brilliantly coloured prints displayed at the 1889 Paris Exposition by the Swiss company, Orell Füssli and Co, won a gold medal, and thrilled those who saw them with their lifelike realism. Only three

The bustle, colour and noise of Piccadilly Circus in central London is vividly brought to life in this photochrome image.

companies – Füssli's own Photoglob in Switzerland, Photochrome in Britain, and the Detroit Printing Company in the USA – were ever licensed to use the "secret" technique, which by 1910 had resulted in more than 13,000 colour images of every corner of Europe, the landmarks of North America, India and North Africa.

Each photochrome involved intensive labour, an artistic eye, and ideally an accurate record of what colours were actually present in the scene portrayed. A film negative was used as the basis for creating a series of lithographic plates – flat pieces of stone quarried in Bavaria and coated with asphaltum, one stone for each colour. The negative had to be hand-retouched for each colour, sometimes fourteen different colours being used, then the stone exposed to sunlight for several hours before being developed with turpentine. Each stone was hand-finished with the additional development of chosen areas and fine pumice powder, before being etched in acid to reveal the image ready for printing. Special semi-transparent inks were then used to transfer the image from the stones onto special smooth paper, and finally each printed image was varnished to bring out its depth and richness.

The British Photochrome Company, with offices in London and Tunbridge Wells, published some 70 photochrome images of the English Lakes, available to the public as prints for framing and as postcards. These and more than 5,000 other photochromes can be seen online at http://www.ushistoricalarchive. com/photochroms/index.html.

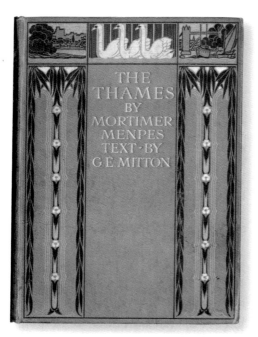

THE TURBAYNE BINDINGS

When they launched the *20 Shilling Series* of coloured books in 1903, A&C Black knew full well that, in order to sell books at such a high price, the look of the book from the outside was just as important as the innovative colour used on the inside.

American-born Albert Angus Turbayne moved to London in the early 1890s and established a close association with the pioneering bindery at The Carlton Studio. By 1903 his William Morris inspired designs were considered to be at the pinnacle of the bookbinder's art. His forte was the combination of exuberant blocking, often in three or

four colours, and beautifully-executed lettering, but one of the bindery's greatest skills was in creating designs that exactly matched the subject of the book. Albert Turbayne always did extensive research into his subject, consulting libraries and illustrated books to find exactly the right elements with which to illustrate each of the Black books.

The design details of the present series of *Memories of Times Past* books pay homage to the skills of the Turbayne Bindery: the designs in the side panels of the cover are derived from the original covers of the Black books, while the decorative elements within the book echo these designs, thus maintaining the theme and feel that Turbayne strove to achieve.

SOURCES, NOTES AND CAPTIONS

The images used to complement the Alfred Heaton Cooper (AHC) paintings come from a wide variety of sources, including books, postcards, museums and libraries. They include photochromes, ephemera, adverts and maps of the period. The numbers refer to the plate numbers.

1 The sketch of charcoal burners preparing a pit is by AHC and is one of a number he produced from 1898 to 1908 in the woodland around Hawkshead, as a record of a dying industry.

2 The plan of the abbey comes from the *Thorough Guide Series* by M.J.B. Baddeley published in 1913, and shows just how close the railway line is to the abbey ruins. The painting of deadly nightshade is from the *Cassell's Encyclopaedia*, "A storehouse of general information," which was only available to readers on subscription.

3 The modern photo of Windermere from Wansfell (left) shows the lake outline exactly as in the AHC painting, and this is echoed in the distorted view of a 1909 map of Windermere from the *Ward Lock Guide*.

4 The bus is the Newby Bridge to Bowness service, photographed in 1920. The hotel rates date from about 1913. Note how the postcard message is the sort of thing that we would send as an email or text message today.

5 The photograph (below left) is of skaters on Windermere on 16 February 1895, and the *Winter Holiday* cover is a first edition of the Arthur Ransome title.

6 The postcard of Windermere ferry dates from 1905, and the map is from the *Baddeley Guide Book*, which was an indispensible item for the Lakeland visitor.

7 The paintings of the laburnums are by A. Fairfax Muckley as reproduced in *Familiar Trees* published by Cassell in 1906. The pergola by the water's edge belonged to the Swan Hotel, Newby Bridge.

8 The postcard in the centre comes from the Museum of Lakeland Life. The larger image (below) is a photochrome showing Windermere and Langdale Pikes.

9 The photochrome (below) shows Grasmere from Red Bank, and the postcard (right) shows Lord Lonsdale at the Grasmere sports in 1910. Note the men with their hounds to the left of the image.

10 The painting is by T. Mower Martin from *Kew Gardens* by A.R. Hope Moncrieff, published in 1908. The line drawing, originally published in black and white, is from *Plant Form and Design*, W. Midgley and A.E.V. Lilley, 1902.

11 The photograph (below left) of the Langdale Pikes and the new Dungeon Ghyll hotel comes from *The English Lakeland*, photographed and published by G.P. Abraham, Keswick. The coloured engraving (right) is the title page of the 1859 book *Lake Scenery of England* by Pyne.

12 Daffodils were a popular subject matter for art nouveau artists. The line drawing (right) is from *Plant Form and Design*, W. Midgley and A.E.V. Lilley, 1902, and the white dead nettle drawing is from *Nature's Own Garden*, published in 1907.

13 The photo (left) shows Stott Park bobbin mill, which was built in 1835. The lathes to make the bobbins were powered by a waterwheel situated behind the buildings. The postcard and the painting (by Sutton Palmer, published in *Rivers and Streams of England*) portray Skelwith Force.

14 On the left we see Rydal Mount as it is today, and as it was painted in a postcard approximately 100 years ago. The colour postcard (right) shows Coleridge's house in a very romantic view of Rydal Water.

15 Note that the photochrome (below right) and the postcard above it are from the same viewpoint as AHC's painting. The photo (left) shows a Rushbearing Festival of 1910. Sarah Nelson started making gingerbread in 1854 in a shop near the church gates using a secret recipe that is still followed today.

16 Look carefully on the envelope and you can see sketches of a cart and horse — these appear as the tradesman's cart in *The Tale of Ginger and Pickles*, 1909. Beatrix Potter's tales are used to teach English in Japan — where they particularly love Peter Rabbit. Many Japanese tourists visit Beatrix Potter's cottage at Hill Top, Near Sawrey, south of Esthwaite Water. The watercolour sketch is of Esthwaite looking towards Coniston fells *c.*1905 by Beatrix Potter.

17 The main plate is entitled "An old street in Hawkshead" but the watercolour (left), painted by AHC in 1902, identifies it by the caption "Ye olde Flag Street". The photograph, by Alfred Pettitt, is also of Flag Street.

18 The photograph (top) shows sheep-shearing at Bainsbank, Middleton, Kirkby Lonsdale, and the postcard shows sheep, presented by Cumberland farmers to Hethersgill chapel, on their way to auction. The detail from a painting (below) is from "Waiting to be Shorn" as published in the *Penrose's Pictorial Annual* of 1906–7.

19 The painting (below left) is by Ernest Haslehust, who produced a large quantity of paintings for the *Beautiful England* series of books published by Blackie and Son. The photograph is of fisherman on Coniston.

20 The photo shows charcoal burners near Haverthwaite, and the two paintings are both by AHC. The one on the left is entitled "Charcoal Burning" and was published by A&C Black in *Wild Lakeland*. The painting on the right of 1908 is entitled "Charcoal Burning at Bouth".

21 Ruskin as photographed in 1869 above an engraving of royal fern by W.J. Linton as published in *Ferns of the English Lake Country*, 1865. Brantwood is shown in the photo, and the image above this depicts char fish.

22 The Black Bull is visible in the top photo of Coniston taken in 1900, and the photo on the bottom right shows the pub as it is today. On the left is Coniston from the church tower as seen in 1920.

23 The photo of a house in Coniston, taken in 1900, shows the same architectural features as the house in the painting. The painting (top) by Turner, is of Tent Lodge, 1818. The view (bottom) is of Coniston Lake, taken from near Brantwood.

24 AHC's pencil sketch and notes (from *Alfred Heaton Cooper, Painter of Landscape* by Jane Renouf) would have been used by the artist later when painting in his studio. In the bottom corner, he clearly identifies the kitchen as being "at the Ship Inn". The photo (top left) shows the Ship Inn as it is today.

25 The two photographs show (left) the distinctive Herdwick sheep, and (left) Yewtree Farm.

26 Wall Barrow Gorge (top) above the Seathwaite stepping-stones illustrates the fast flow of water at this point. Wonderful Walker's grave stone is positioned in a shady spot in the graveyard of Seathwaite Church (below).

27 The photo (below) is of Greenodd in the big freeze of 1895, a year that saw people skating on the frozen waters of Windermere.

28 The painting is a watercolour painted by Berenger Beer entitled "When daffodils begin to peer". The photographic image of the daffodil comes from *Penrose's Pictorial Annual* 1910–11.

29 AHC's 1920 painting is of Coniston Hunt on Red Screes. The photo of the Blencathra hounds at Newlands (left) echoes the composition of Heaton's painting.

30 The modern photo of Wastwater from Strands is taken from roughly the same view as AHC's painting; the shoreline still follows a similar path. Great Gable is in view in the photo (top right) showing the Head of Wastwater.

31 The images of mountaineering equipment come from *The Book of the Home: A comprehensive guide on all matters pertaining to the household.* The photo shows a climber on Scafell pinnacle, 1920.

32 Sprinkling Tarn and Great Gable is the title of the dramatic painting by AHC. The photo (left) shows the head of Wastwater with Great Gable behind. The right-hand photo is of Hugh Walpole and his dog.

33 The drawing of Wastwater by Edmund New was published in *The English Lakes* by F. Brabant in 1902. The map is from the same book, and the photograph dates from 1910.

34 The photo (left) of Wasdale Church, taken in 1910, shows the same yew tree that AHC painted. The top photo, taken in 1920, is from the opposite end of the church. The painting of the yew tree in a churchyard is from *Familiar Trees*, published by Cassell in 1907.

35 The painting (bottom right) is of Styhead Pass to Wastwater by AHC. Styhead Tarn (middle) is just below the pass. A climber practises his art at the stables of the Wastwater Hotel (top). The photo (right) shows Napes Needle.

36 Will Ritson (left), owner of the Huntsman's Inn, and Wasdale Head from Wastwater (photo).

37 The photo shows Black Sail Youth hostel as it is today. The painting by AHC is of Black Sail Pass. Ennerdale Bridge, the nearest village at the western end, has a churchyard that was the setting for a poem called "The Brothers" by Wordsworth. The story is that a man comes back from years at sea as a sailor and asks the vicar about a particular grave that has no stone on it. By the description it turns out to have been his brother whom he hasn't communicated with since he went to sea.

38 Two slightly different views of Pillar Rock by AHC. That on the left was painted in 1905 and the other in 1910.

39 The colour engraving by Pyne, dating from 1859, is titled Lowes Water – another example of how names change subtly over the years.

40 Note the postman with a hook in the old photo of Coniston Post Office (right) and that the postman from near Arnside (left) has a special rack on the front of his bicycle to carry post.

41 The men in the photo are carrying bottles filled with paraffin and aniseed which was poured onto pads that were dragged along the ground to lay the trail for the hounds. Pyne's colour engraving of 1859 shows almost the same view as AHC's painting.

42 Ernest Haslehust's painting of Scale Force (top) was published in 1910 in *The English Lakes*. The photo (left) dates from 1902.

43 The photo of Buttermere Church (top) was taken in 1910. The coach ride on the Borrowdale and Honister round (right) demonstrates just how scary the experience must have been.

44 The meadowsweet (top left) was drawn by Mabel E. Step for publication in *Wayside and Woodland Blossoms*, 1909. All the other images are different views of Honister Pass and the painting by Haslehust shows the Pass at dawn.

45 The Borrowdale Yews as they appear today (right) and a beautiful photochrome of Borrowdale in full leaf.

46 Lodore Falls are "foaming with fury" in the photochrome (centre), while Lodore by moonlight is illustrated in the postcard (right).

47 The postcard (left) shows Watendlath in around 1910. The decorative image of Derwentwater (below) is from the 1903–4 *Penrose's Pictorial Annual*.

48 The detail from a painting by Anders Zorn (top right), as reproduced in *Penrose's Pictorial Annual* 1906–7, must almost certainly have been used as reference by AHC for the painting – the poses are almost identical, and the dates tally. The image at the foot of the page is a photochrome of Derwentwater.

49 The large photo of Bowder Stone was taken in 1902. The advert for the pencil works comes from *A Pictorial and Descriptive Guide to The English Lake District*, which was in its 17th edition in 1913–14.

50 Canon Hardwicke Drummond Rawnsley (left) was Vicar of Crosthwaite Church when the drawing of the church (right) by Joseph Pennell was published in *Highways and Byways in the Lake District* in 1901.

51 Pyne's colour engraving of 1859, showing the "Druid" circle, captures the supposedly sinister atmosphere of the place, as does the earlier 1835 engraving (inset). Castlerigg is not a true circle; it has a flattened face on the north east side, and inside the eastern end of the circle a group of ten stones forms a rectangular enclosure.

52 The Thomas Smith engraving (top) of 1767 is entitled "View of Derwentwater". The painting of Derwentwater from Friar's Crag is by Haslehust, 1920.

53 Various views of Castle Rock. The engraving (left) dates from the 1830s. The photo shows St John's Church.

54 Derwentwater and the Falls of Lodore painted by Turner around 1797. The "Claude Glass" (right), named after the 17th-century landscape artist Claude Lorrain, consisted of a convex mirror which concentrated a panorama into a small image, and a sepia-coloured glass which emphasised tonal values.

55 The image of the osprey in flight comes from the *Harmsworth Natural History*, 1910; the church is St Bega's.

56 Mirehouse in the Victorian age (below), and in the present day (inset), with an image of Tennyson. The painting of Bassenthwaite and Skiddaw (right) is by Ernest Haslehust.

57 The aqueduct is 96 metres long and was constructed by the Manchester Corporation Water Works in 1897. The lake once had a high count of *Cryptospiridium* that infected a child in Bolton, Lancashire. The engraving of Raven Crag (top) is by Francis Towne. The illustration of the raven is from *Harmsworth's Natural History*, 1910.

58 Two images of Striding Edge (top), one a painting by AHC, the other a photograph from *Hutchinson's Beautiful Britain*. The photochrome below shows Thirlmere and Helvellyn.

59 The remains of Mardale are visible in the photo (left) of Haweswater from Rough Crag. The Pyne engraving of 1859 (centre) shows Haweswater and Wallergill Force. The Dun Bull is shown in the 1908 photograph (right).

60 AHC painted Shap Abbey in the context of the Fells (below) and this painting was published in *Wild Lakeland* in 1922.

61 AHC's painting (below) is called "Ullswater Mount", while the 1859 Pyne engraving shows Ullswater from Gobarrow (note old spelling) Park.

62 Ullswater as portrayed by William Green (top) contrasts with the more romantic views. The postcard (bottom right) shows Stybarrow Crag.

63 Silver Strand on a stormy day by AHC complements his painting of the same view after sunset.

64 The view of Ullswater in a decorative frame (right) matches the mood of AHC's painting. The photo was taken by C.S. Best and featured in *Penrose's Pictorial Annual* 1906–7.

65 The gorse illustration is by Mabel E. Step, and was published in 1909. The photochrome shows Ullswater, hotel and lake.

66 The painting (top left) is of Lady Anne Clifford. The photographs (bottom and centre right) show the river in front of the castle has moved over the years – it is absent in the colour modern-day photo, whereas the photograph from *Hutchinson's Beautiful Britain* (below) shows the river exactly as in AHC's painting.

67 The photo (top) shows Angle Tarn and Eastern Fells, and the painting (below) by AHC is called "Wild Ponies, Angle Tarn, Patterdale".

68 The photo (left) shows the Laal Ratty train some time in the 1920s. The shot of the group in a carriage (below) was taken in 1908. The house (right) is Dalegarth Hall.

69 The photochrome (bottom) shows Blea Tarn, and the 1859 Pyne colour engraving shows the Langdale Pikes.

70 The title of the Heaton painting (left) is "The Abode of the Solitary, Blea Tarn", and was published in *Wild Lakeland* in 1922.

71 Pyne's 1859 engraving of Brotherswater, showing three men (brothers?) skating on the lake, illustrates beautifully the story of how the lake got its name. The photo (left) shows the Kirkstone Inn in 1890.

72 The illustration of heathers is by C.F. Newall, from *Plant-Life*, published in 1915 by A&C Black. The photo shows Easedale Tarn.

73 Slater's Bridge (top right) today, and Blea Tarn House, Little Langdale (below). The painting of the dog rose is by C.F. Newall; from *Plant-Life*, published in 1915 by A&C Black.

74 The engraving of Elterwater is by John Ernes and dates from 1794.

75 The art nouveau design contrasts with the stark image of the char fish from *Harmsworth's Natural History*.

The A&C Black Colour Books, Colin Inman, Werner Shaw, 1990

Alfred Heaton Cooper, Painter of Landscape, Jane Renouf, Red Bank Press, 1997

Alpine Flora, Coloured Vade Mecum, L. Schröter, Albert Raustein, 7th edition, 1900

300 Art Nouveau Designs and Motifs, edited by Carol Belanger, Grafton, 1983

Beatrix Potter. Her Art and Inspiration, National Trust, 2004

Birds of Britain, J. Lewis Bonhote, A&C Black, 1907

Blacks Guide to The English Lakes Books, edited by Gordon Home, A&C Black, 1913

Book of the Home, A Comprehensive Guide on all Matters Pertaining to the Household, edited by Mrs C.E. Humphry, Greasham, 6 volumes, ND

Cassell's Encyclopaedia, A Storehouse of General Information, Cassell & Co Ltd, 8 volumes, ND

A Celebration of 40 Years of Lake District Life, edited by Hilary Gray, Pelham Books, 1991

Companion Guide to the Lake District, Frank Welsh, Collins, 1989

Cumberland and Westmorland, Norman Nicholson, Robert Hale, 1949

Cumberland Heritage, Molly Lefebure, Victor Gollancz, 1970

Cumbria Memories, John Marsh and John Garbutt, Sutton, 2000

Cumbrian Discovery, Molly Lefebure, Victor Gollancz, 1977

The English Lake District, Baddeley's Thorough Guide Series, No 17, M.J.B. Baddeley, Thomas Nelson and Sons, 1913

The English Lakes, Wordsworth Country, painted by Alfred Heaton Cooper, Salmon Ltd, 7th edition, 2002

The English Lakes, pictures by Ernest Haslehust, described by A.G. Bradley, Blackie and Son Ltd, 1910

The English Lakes, F. G. Brabant, with illustrations by Edmund New, Methuen, 1902

Familiar Trees, G.S. Boulger, Cassell and Company Limited, 1906

Family Album, Edwardian Life in the Lake Counties, John Satchell, Sutton, 1996

Fellwalking With Wainwright, Alfred Wainwright & Derry Brabbs, Michael Joseph, 1985

The Gateway to the English Lakeland, photographed and published by G.P. Abraham, Keswick, ND

Grasmere Sports: The First 150 Years, Roy Lomas, M.T.P. Publications, 2002

Harmsworth Natural History, volumes 1–3, Carmelite House, 1910

Hawkshead Revisited, John Dixon, Helm Press, 2000

Highways and Byways in the Lake District. A.G. Bradley, with illustrations by Joseph Pennell, Macmillan and Co Ltd, 1901

Highways and Hedges, painted by Berenger Benger, described by Herbert A. Morrah, A&C Black, 1911

A History of Man in the Lake District, William Rollinson, J.M. Dent, 1967

Hutchinson's Beautiful Britain, edited by Walter Hutchinson, ND

The Illustrated History of Colour Photography, Jack Coote, Fountain Press, 1993

Italian Lakes, Richard Bagot, A&C Black, 1905

Kew Gardens, A.R. Hope Moncrieff, painted by T. Mower Martin, A&C Black, 1908

Land of the Lakes, Melvyn Bragg, Secker and Warburg, 1983

The Lake Counties of 100 Years Ago, John Marsh and John Garbutt, Sutton, 1994

The Lake District, National Trust Histories, Chris Barringer, Willow Books/Collins with The National Trust, 1983

The Lake District: A Prose Anthology, Norman Nicholson, Robert Hale, 1977

The Lake District and its County, John Wyatt, Robert Hale, 2004

The Lake District at Work, Past and Present, J.D. Marshall and M. Davies-Shiel, David and Charles, 1971

The Lake Scenery of England, J.B. Pyne, Drawn on Stone by T. Picken Day and Son, London, first published 1859

The Lakers, Norman Nicholson, Robert Hale, 1955

A Literary Guide to the Lake District, Grevel Lindop, Chatto and Windus, 1993

The Maid of Buttermere, Melvyn Bragg, Hodder & Stoughton, 1987

Nature's Own Garden, written and illustrated by Maud U. Clarke, J.M. Dent, 1907

Our Darlings, The Children's Treasury of Pictures and Stories, John F. Shaw & Co, ND

Penrose's Pictorial Annual, various from 1900

A Pictorial and Descriptive Guide to The English Lake District, Illustrated Guide Book, Ward Lock and Co, 17th edition, c.1913–14

Plant Form and Design, W. Midgley and A.E.V. Lilley, 1902

Plant life, Charles A. Hall, A&C Black, 1915

Portrait of the Lakes, Norman Nicholson, Robert Hale Ltd, 1963

Rivers and Streams of England, described by A.G. Bradley, painted by Sutton Palmer, A&C Black, ND

Tales and Legends of the English Lakes, Armistead Wilson, Marshall & Co. 1891

Turner's Golden Visions, C. Lewis Hind, T.C.&E.C. Jack, London, ND

Victorian and Edwardian Fashion, Alison Gernsheim, Dover Books, 1981

Wayside and Woodland Blossoms, Edward & Mabel Step, Frederick Warne & Co, 1906

Wild Lakeland, MacKenzie MacBride, with illustrations by Alfred Heaton Cooper, A&C Black, 1922

The Windermere Ferry, History, Boats, Ferrymen and Passengers, Dick White, Helm Press, 2002

THE TIMES PAST ARCHIVE

The *Memories of Times Past* series would be inconceivable without the massive Times Past Archive, a treasury of books, magazines, atlases, postcards and printed ephemera from the "golden age" of colour printing between 1895 and 1915.

From the time several years ago when the project was first conceived, the collecting of material from all over the world has proceeded in earnest. As well as a complete set of the ninety-two A&C Black 20 Shilling colour books, which are the inspiration for the series, the Archive houses full sets of period *Baedeker* and *Murray's Guides*, almost every colour-illustrated travel book from illustrious publishing houses like Dent, Jack, Cassell, Blackie and Chatto & Windus, and a massive collection of reference works with colour plates on subjects from railways and military uniforms to wild flowers and birds' eggs.

The Archive also contains complete runs of all the important periodicals of the time that contained colour illustrations, including the pioneering *Penrose's Pictorial Annual: An Illustrated Review of the Graphic Arts*; the first-ever British colour magazine, *Colour*; ladies' magazines like *Ladies' Field* and *The Crown*; and more popular titles like *The Connoisseur* and *The London Magazine*.

These years were vintage years for atlas publishing, and the Times Past Archive contains such gems as Keith Johnston's *Royal Atlas of Modern Geography*, *The Harmsworth Atlas*, Bartholomew's *Survey Atlas of England and Wales*, and the *Illustrated and Descriptive Atlas of The British Empire*.

Last but not least, the Archive includes a wealth of smaller items — souvenirs, postcards, tickets, programmes, catalogues, posters, and all the colourful ephemera with which the readers of the original 20 Shilling books would have been familiar.

THE TIMES PAST WEBSITE

The website to accompany this project can be found at *www. memoriesoftimespast.com*, where you will find further information about the birth and development of the project, together with the complete original texts of titles published to date. There is also an area where you can take part in discussions raised by readers of the books who want to take their interest further and share their memories and passions with others. The website will start small and elegant, as you would expect of an "Edwardian website", but it will gradually become what you and we together make it, a place for devotees of art and culture from a century ago to meet and be inspired.

ACKNOWLEDGEMENTS

We would like to thanks the following people for help and advice: Jeff Cowton, Ann Lambert and John Coombe of The Wordsworth Trust, Dove Cottage, Grasmere; Tanya Flower and staff at The Armitt Collection, Ambleside, Cumbria; Peggy and Jim Foster, Brookhouse, Lancaster; Elizabeth Brown, Coniston; Anne Hall, Coniston; Kendal Public Library, Kendal, Cumbria; Rosemary Park of Elterwater; Myles Sandys of Graythwaite, near Hawkshead; Vickie Slowe, the Ruskin Museum, Coniston; John Spedding, Mirehouse, Bassenthwaite, Cumbria; Maurice Steele, The Old Smithy, Eskdale, Cumbria; *Westmorland Gazette*, Kendal; Pamela and Dick White, Stodday, Lancaster.

PICTURE CREDITS

l = left, r = right, b = below, t = top, m = middle
Page references refer to pages in this title.

A&C Black Colour Books, Colin Inman, Werner Shaw, 1990, page 166(t)
Abbot Hall Art Gallery, Kendal, plate 62(t)
Alfred Heaton Cooper, Painter of Landscape, Jane Renouf, Red Bank Press, 1997, all images on pages 11, 12 and 13, and plates 1(b), 16(tl), 17(l), 24(tr & b), 29(b), 38(l & r), 63(b)
Beatrix Potter, Her Art and Inspiration, National Trust, 2004, plate 16: Landscape of Esthwaite (b) © Frederick Warne & Co., Ltd, 1905, envelope addressed to Beatrix Potter © Courtesy of the National Trust.
Bill Birkett, plates 26(t), 30(l), 36(b), 39(r), 43(bl), 45(m), 63(bl), 68(r), 70(r)
The Black Bull Hotel, Coniston, plate 22(br)
The Brantwood Trust, plate 21(br)
Cumbria County Libraries, plate 50(tl), 52(tr)
Cumbria Image Bank (www.cumbriaimagebank.co.uk), plates 9(br), 13(r), 18(br), 19(t), 21(tl), 25(tl & br) 60(t & br)
Cumbria Lakes (www.cumbrialakes.org), plates 22(bl), 25(bl), 26(ml), 33(tl), 34(t & l), 41(m), 43(tr), 47(l), 53(tl), 68(tl), 73(br), 74(ml)
Cumbria Memories, John Marsh and John Garbutt, Sutton, 2000, pages 4(b), 19(b), and plates 15(l), 27(l), 29(l), 31(r), 40(l), 43(br), 59(br)
Family Album, Edwardian Life in the Lake Counties, John Satchell, Sutton, 1996, pages 3(r), 5(r), 9(l), and plates 49(b), 68(b)
Heaton Cooper Studio, Grasmere, plate 20(r)
The Illustrated History of Colour Photography, Jack Coote, Fountain Press, 1993, page 166(bl)
The Lake Counties of 100 Years Ago, John Marsh and John Garbutt, Sutton, 1994, page 10(t), and plates 7(bl), 17(r), 18(t), 20(t), 27(b), 30(b), 40(r), 44(br)
The Lake District at Work, Past and Present, J.D. Marshall and M. Davies-Shiel, David and Charles, 1971, plate 13 (l)
The Lake District, National Trust Histories, Chris Barringer, Willow Books/Collins with The National Trust, 1983, plate 57(t)
The Museum of Lakeland Life, plates 8(tm), 14(tr & tl), 15(t), 32(l), 46(r), 47(m), 52(l), 53(b)
National Railway Museum and Science and Society photo library, pages 1(r), and 2(t & l) and plate 62 (l)
The Ship Inn, Coniston, plate 24(tl)
South Lakes website (www.southlakes-uk.co.uk), plates 1(tr), 4(br), 9(l), 22(t), 23(r), 68(t), 71(bl)
John Spedding, plate 56(b)
The Swan Hotel, Newby Bridge (www.swanhotel.com), plate 4
300 Art Nouveau Designs and Motifs, edited by Carol Belanger, Grafton, 1983, plate 75(b)
Tuck's postcards, pages 1(l), 165(br), 166(t) and plates 9(l), 53(br), 62(br), 70(bl)
Tullie House Museum and Art Gallery, Carlisle, plate 66(tl)
Victoria and Albert Museum, plate 54(r)
Victorian and Edwardian Fashion, Alison Gernsheim, Dover Books, 1981, page 9(r)